How to
Invest in
BONDS

BY HUGH C. SHERWOOD
The Journalistic Interview

How to Invest in BONDS

Hugh C. Sherwood

McGraw-Hill Book Company

New York • St. Louis • San Francisco • Düsseldorf • Mexico • Montreal
Panama • Paris • São Paulo • Tokyo • Toronto

copyw 7/1974

IV.

Contents

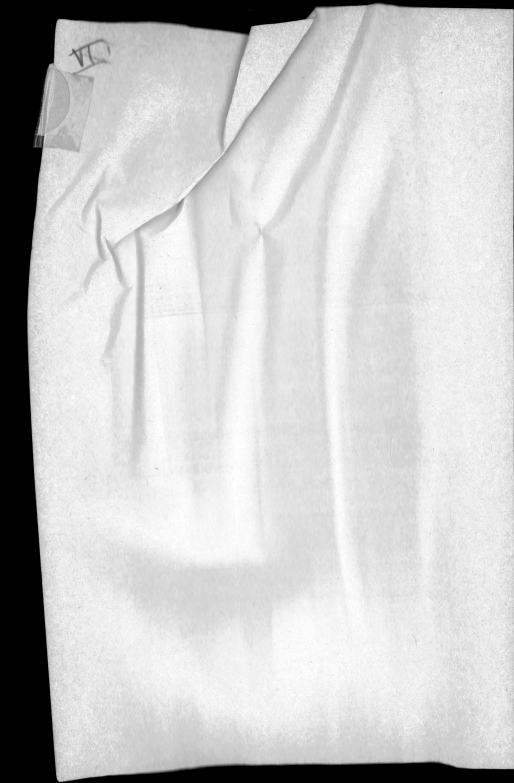

Preface (2 dys)

This book is not written for the professional bond analyst, dealer or trader. Rather it is written for both the average investor and the novice. It seeks to provide these investors with a basic working knowledge of different kinds of bonds, bond funds and bond markets.

You will not learn how to make a million dollars in twelve easy lessons. Life is rarely that simple. And even if it were, I do not believe in formulas that promise easy success in an uncertain world. If the book increases its readers' knowledge of bonds and helps them conserve their financial resources, obtain a good income from them and possibly increase their size, it will have served its purpose.

In writing this book, I am indebted to Charles E. Walsh, vice president of the fixed-income trading department of The First Boston Corporation, for making a number of sage observations, which are included throughout the book; H. Russell Fraser, vice president of the corporate finance department of Standard & Poor's Corporation, for enlarging my knowledge of how bonds are rated and for reviewing Chapter 3; Ronald D. Bechky, assistant vice president of the convertible bond trading department of Merrill Lynch, Pierce, Fenner & Smith, for providing cogent commentary on convertible bonds and for reviewing Chapter 6; Alan W. Leeds, a partner of L.F. Rothschild & Company, for providing invaluable information about how bonds are bought and sold and for reviewing Chapter 10; and F. Douglas Harrell, sales manager of the bond funds department of Merrill Lynch, Pierce, Fenner & Smith, for enhancing my knowledge of bond funds and for reviewing Chapter 11. Finally, I wish to thank Joseph M. Ryan, an old college friend who is now a bond salesman with Blyth Eastman Dillon, for answering a number of queries about bonds and bond markets.

I have enjoyed writing this book and have learned a great deal in the process. I hope you will be similarly served.

—HUGH C. SHERWOOD
White Plains, New York

Chapter 1

$$ges\ frm\ pg\ 1\ to\ pg\ 8 = 8\ pgs,$$

The World of Bonds: Today and Tomorrow

In October 1971 *Fortune* published an article that now seems both prophetic and the beneficiary of hindsight. The article was entitled "A Bad New Era for Common Stocks." And it contained so much meat that it is worth quoting a few of its sentences.

"We are," it said, "in fact, we have been for some time, in a new era on Wall Street; the casino has changed the rules. Under the new rules, players still run large risks, but payoffs to the winners are relatively meager . . .

"This bad new era seems to have begun around the end of 1965 . . . the principal reason for dating the bad new era back to 1965 is that we know, in retrospect, that the year ushered in an era of persistent inflation. There is a well-known legend to the effect that inflation helps common stock prices; in fact, it is bad news for stocks. Actually, it is calamitous news . . .

"To suggest that stocks have had it is not to project another 1929. There will still be broad-based rallies, and individual issues may soar . . . But over-all, returns will be a lot lower than those prevailing in the first two post-war decades. Stocks will be competing strenuously with bonds —whose returns will be substantially more attractive than they were during the lush post-war years. Bond yields will increasingly function as a kind of ceiling on stock prices."*

To grasp the article's full import, you must bear in mind that throughout the 1950s and 1960s investors were repeatedly told, in newspaper stories and magazine articles, in speeches and seminars, that common stocks represented one of the few good hedges against inflation. They were advised that, if they would just put their money in common stocks, their wealth would probably grow faster than the purchasing power of the dollar declined. If, however, they were so foolish as to leave their money in savings banks or to put it in bonds, mortgages or other so-called fixed-income investments, they would inevitably lose out to inflation.

In its well-documented article, *Fortune* strongly questioned this whole thesis. Inflation, the magazine emphasized, usually brings about a rise in interest rates. And as is common knowledge in Wall Street, high interest rates tend to depress common stock prices. That's because many investors tend to sell their stocks and put their money in bonds and other fixed-income securities.

Even if all this were not true, common stocks have never been a perfect hedge against inflation. To be sure, many investors have made small fortunes by investing in them. But exhaustive studies done by the University of Chicago's Center for Research in Security Prices show that if an investor had bought all the stocks listed on the New York Stock Exchange at the beginning of 1926 and held them until the

*Reprinted by permission of *Fortune* magazine.

— chpt 1 — 3.

end of 1974, he would have enjoyed an average annual return on his investment, before taxes, 8.5 percent. Importantly, this return would have included both appreciation in the prices of the stocks and the dividends paid on them, and it would have assumed that the dividends were reinvested.

A return of 8.5 percent is not a bad return. On the other hand, it does not correspond to the 8.8 percent increase in the Consumer Price Index that occurred during 1973. Nor is it much, if any, better than the interest rates that have sometimes been paid on high-quality bonds over the past few years.

Furthermore, a return of 8.5 percent is not a sure return. Rather it is an average return. And many investors have not done as well as the average.

Indeed, in recent years it has not been easy for anyone to make money in the stock market. In 1973, reports Interactive Data Corporation, only 13 percent of all the stocks listed on the New York Stock Exchange rose in price. More than one-half fell by upward of 30 percent.

So the typical investor not only did not achieve a return of 8.5 percent that year, he did not achieve any return at all. He lost money—quite a bit of it.

Does all this mean that bonds are a better hedge against inflation than stocks? Not necessarily. Potentially, stocks are a better hedge against inflation than bonds can ever hope to be. Furthermore, the high interest rates that bonds have recently returned may fall sharply, if not tomorrow then next month or next year or the year thereafter. The prices of common stocks may rise almost across the board.

What all this does mean is that, as matters have recently stood, bonds have been a very viable alternative to stocks. They have demanded the attention of virtually all investors, institutional and individual alike. And not surprisingly, they have received such attention.

Slowly, but almost inexorably, institutions like insurance companies and corporate pension funds have begun to channel more and more of their funds into bonds. In 1973, says the New York Stock Exchange, private pension funds bought a mere $3.6 billion worth of corporate stock, only about one-half as much as they had purchased the preceding year. At the same time, they increased their net purchases of corporate bonds from $1.6 billion to $2.8 billion.

Kaiser Industries is reported to have put one-third of its pension fund in fixed-income investments. And Trans Union Corporation is said to have put all of its pension fund there. As this is written, many investment experts see no end to this trend in sight.

Individuals have also been flocking to the bond market —and in what may be record numbers. In 1970 New Jersey Bell Telephone issued $100 million worth of bonds that returned the highest yield—9.35 percent—of any security ever put out by a subsidiary of American Telephone & Telegraph up until that time.* Merrill Lynch handled some $27 million worth of the issue and sold about two-thirds of this amount to individuals. This is an unusually high figure in a market that has always been heavily dominated by institutions.

Indeed, the growth in individual participation in the bond market has been so great that twenty-four million Americans now own bonds of one kind or another. This is not many less than the thirty or so million who own common stocks. And to meet the increasing demand from individuals, bond funds have sprung into existence at such a rate that it has been almost impossible to keep track of them.

*In 1974 the Mountain States Telephone Company, another AT&T subsidiary, issued $175 million worth of bonds that initially yielded 9.91 percent.

chpt 1 (cont)

5.

Of course, these are not the only important trends in today's bond market. Several others are worth mentioning.

Thus, in recent years there has been a tremendous increase in all kinds of debt—federal, state and corporate. Since 1947 alone, the total value of bonds outstanding has increased more than three-fold.

What's more, most signs indicate that the trend will continue. The evidence shows that there will be sharp increases in overall borrowings in 1974 and that corporate borrowings will probably run at a record level.

Looking further ahead, James J. Needham, chairman of the New York Stock Exchange, reports that American business may need more than $3 trillion in new capital between the present time and 1985. Naturally, it won't seek to meet all its needs by issuing bonds. It will generate a great deal of cash from its own profits. It will obtain some more by issuing new stock. And it will obtain more yet by borrowing from commercial banks. Even so, a considerable portion of its needs will have to be met through bond issues.

Together with the marked increase in the need for capital has come a marked increase in the secondary market for bonds. Thus, once a bond has been issued and sold, it may be sold again and, if it is, the sale is made in what's called the secondary or after market.

Observes Charles E. Walsh, vice president of the fixed-income trading department of The First Boston Corporation: "In the last ten years, there has not only been a tremendous increase in the volume of business done in the secondary market, but also a tremendous increase in the size of the typical purchases made by institutions. Furthermore, these institutions are much more active than once was the case. They are less apt to buy bonds and hold them until they mature. They are more apt to seek profits by buying bonds and then selling them from time to time, just as they periodically buy and sell common stocks."

These are some of the important recent trends in the bond market. But what of the future? In particular, will the interest rates paid on bonds remain at or near their recent levels, which have been very high by historical standards?

I will not venture to make a prediction on this point. Even if I were an economist, I would hesitate to do so. This very year, many economists have erred badly in predicting what would happen to interest rates.

I do not say this to malign economists, who, after all, often disagree among themselves. I merely wish to indicate that the task of economic forecasting is still an art, not a science.

Nonetheless, two observations should be made about interest rates. First, many economists think these rates will remain high. Says Tilford C. Gaines, senior vice president and economist of Manufacturers Hanover Trust: "For the foreseeable future, a return to the interest-rate levels that this country has enjoyed historically would seem to be a most remote possibility." Second, it seems likely that the economists will be proved correct, at least as long as inflation remains severe and persistent. There is widespread, although not universal, agreement that there is a relation between severe inflation and high interest rates. Even if both should fall, they may not fall far.

From everything that has been said so far, it may seem as if the world of bonds were a healthy, bubbling world. But nothing could be further from the truth. As First Boston's Charles Walsh recently put it: "I would call the bond market viable rather than healthy."

So much depends on how you look at this world. If you purchased bonds in the summer of 1974, the world may indeed seem rosy. Interest rates were high then. And, as you may know, interest rates and bond prices move in opposite directions. If and when interest rates on new bonds fall, the prices of old bonds will rise. And you will

—or should—win in two ways: you will have locked in a high rate of interest for as long as you care to own your bonds. And when prices rise, you can then sell the bonds, achieving a capital gain.

But if you have owned bonds for many years, you may be much less happy. You probably bought your bonds when interest rates were much lower. You are still earning the same old interest. And as new bonds have come out, carrying higher interest rates, the prices of your bonds have fallen so as to make their yields competitive with those on the new ones. If you now have to sell your bonds, you may well suffer a sharp loss in the value of your investment.

If you belong to an investment banking firm that underwrites new bond issues, you may be unhappier yet. For today competition is severe and profits slim. Furthermore, the bond market is sharply depressed in price from the levels that prevailed throughout most of the 1960s.

Even so, it remains a colorful world, replete with its own language and ways of doing business. It is a world where "market in the shoot" means bond prices are dropping fast and where well-known companies are commonly known by irreverent nicknames, a world where "Lollipops" stands for Long Island Lighting Company and "Fat City" designates First National City Bank.

Let us now turn to what is likely to be of immediate, practical use to people interested in investing in bonds. In so doing, bear in mind the significant information we have learned from this chapter:

According to the most definitive, long-range study ever done, the average pretax return on investments in common stocks has been 8.5 percent annually. In recent years, the average annual return on high-quality bonds has often approached, equaled or even exceeded this level and thus made bonds a viable alternative to persons trying to keep abreast of inflation. So long as inflation remains high and persistent and so long as the demand for capital remains intense, it seems likely, although not certain, that the returns on bonds will not fall too many percentage points from their recent levels. Certainly the return of the day when long-term corporate bonds returned only 4 percent does not seem close at hand.

End of chpt 1

goes fm pg. 9 to 28...

Chapter 2

The ABC's of Bonds

Bonds are widely considered the most conservative of all investments. To understand why, it is only necessary to understand the nature of a bond itself.

When an institution or an individual buys a bond, he makes a loan to whatever organization issued it. In return, the issuer promises to repay the loan at a certain specified date in the future and in the meantime to pay the buyer a guaranteed rate of interest.

Thus a bond is, in effect, a promissory note or IOU. Whoever buys a bond becomes a creditor of the government, governmental agency or corporation that issued it. The proof of the agreement is engraved on the bond itself. Thus, if you have ever seen one, you know that it contains a serial number, a principal amount, a date on which the principal amount will be repaid, an interest rate, plus the name of the issuer.

How different, then, a bond is from a stock. When an individual buys a stock, he does not become a creditor. Rather he becomes an owner.

The corporation whose stock he has purchased promises him nothing. Hopefully, of course, it will do well, increasing its earnings from year to year. In such case, the price of its stock is apt to go up, and it is apt to pay its owners bigger and bigger dividends.

There is no guarantee, however, that this will happen. In fact, the reverse could take place. In such case, the price of the stock may plunge, the corporation may not pay any dividends on it at all, and its owner may find his investment worth only a fraction of what he paid for it.

Like a stock, a bond may fluctuate in price. If its owner has to sell it before it matures, he, too, may lose a great deal of money. But if he holds the bond until it matures, he will almost always get back the amount of money indicated on the face of the bond.

To be sure, a bond issue sometimes goes into default. In other words, the issuer is unable to pay principal, interest or both. But defaults are rare. And when they occur, bondholders have a prior claim on all the issuer's assets. As a result, the issuer must sell or otherwise dispose of its plant, equipment and other assets, then divide up the proceeds among its bondholders in accordance with what it owes them. Stockholders may get only a small part of the proceeds or even nothing at all. For this reason, bonds are sometimes referred to as *senior securities.*

If all this sounds as if bonds were an inherently better investment than stocks, it isn't necessarily so. If a company's profits soar, a stockholder is very likely to benefit through an increase in the price of the stock, an increase in the size of the dividends or both. A bondholder, on the other hand, rarely benefits from rising profits.

All this is another way of saying that stocks and bonds

are different animals. Each has advantages and disadvantages the other doesn't.

Now who issues bonds? There are four major kinds of issuers. The first consists of corporations, and the bonds they issue are known as corporates. The second consists of state or local governments or other public bodies on the state or local level, and the bonds they issue are known as municipals. The third issuer is the United States government, and its issues are called governments. The fourth issuer consists of various agencies of the United States government.

The government issues its bonds without much outside aid, and its agencies do so in a special fashion that will be described in Chapter 9. Corporations and state and local governments, on the other hand, issue bonds with the help of a special kind of banker known as an <u>investment banker.</u>
An investment banker agrees to buy an issuer's bonds and resell them to the public. In fact, he does a great deal more. He advises his client on how much money can be raised in the bond market and on what rate of interest will have to be paid. He also agrees to advertise the bonds and to arrange for their distribution throughout the country and perhaps overseas.

If a bond issue is very small, a single investment banker may *float* the issue. If it is very large, a number of investment bankers may join forces. In this case, they form a *syndicate* or *underwriting group.*

To give you some idea of the variation in the size of these groups, a syndicate of only five investment bankers recently announced that it was marketing $35 million worth of bonds for the Public Service Company of Oklahoma. On the very same day, a syndicate of no fewer than 171 investment bankers announced that it was floating more than $349 million worth of bonds for the City of New York.

Many times, corporations would prefer not to issue

bonds at all. Often, they would much rather issue stock. It is easy to understand one reason why when you recall that when a company sells stock, it commits itself to nothing. When it sells bonds, however, it not only promises to repay the amount it borrows, but also to pay interest along the way. In this sense it is more expensive to issue bonds than stock.

Nonetheless, at any given point in time, it may not be feasible to issue stock. For example, a company may be a private one whose owners do not wish to share their profits with other owners. Or it may be relatively unknown and stand little chance that a stock issue will be well received. Or the stock market may be relatively inactive and unhealthy.

Whatever the situation, companies, governments and other public agencies issue bonds all the time. In fact, they issue them in such numbers and such amounts that the bond market dwarfs the stock market in size many times over. In a typical year, the ratio of new bond issues to new stock issues may be five or even ten to one.

Furthermore, these organizations issue bonds for all kinds of purposes. They may wish to raise money to build a new factory or to buy new equipment. Or to acquire another company. Or to pay off the owners of older bond issues. Or to reimburse other creditors.

Sometimes a combination of reasons is involved. For example, in 1974 TRW Inc. issued $75 million worth of bonds in order to pay off long-term bank debt incurred in foreign lands, to pay off short-term bank debt incurred in this country and to retire commercial paper.

Who buys bonds? Institutional investors, such as banks, charitable foundations, colleges, insurance companies, and pension funds, have long dominated the bond market. Of course, as we saw in Chapter 1, individual investors have recently come forward in much greater numbers than they did during the 1950s and 1960s.

Still and all, the bond market is basically an institutional market and is likely to remain that way for as long as we can foresee. Even in the aggregate, individuals simply do not have sufficient investment funds to meet the borrowing needs of the nation's corporations and governmental bodies.

The fact is, institutional demand for bonds is so great that an underwriter will sometimes tell a client that he can persuade just one or two big institutional investors to purchase an entire issue. When this happens, the underwriter is said to have made a *private placement.* In recent years such placements have occasionally accounted for more than one-third of the sales of all new corporate issues.

But usually an underwriter or syndicate buys the bonds from its client, then resells them to the institutional and general public for a slightly higher price. Sometimes an underwriter will negotiate the terms of such a deal with the client. More often, underwriters or groups of underwriters make competitive bids to underwrite a bond issue. In the latter case, the underwriter that enables the client to pay the lowest rate of interest wins the bid.

Bonds are issued in certain *denominations.* These denominations may be as small as $100 or as large as $5,000 and occasionally many times larger. Ordinarily, however, bonds are issued in denominations of $1,000. Thus it is usually assumed that $1,000 is a bond's *principal amount* or *face value.* It is the amount that the borrower will repay when a bond matures.

Curiously enough, however, bond dealers, magazines and newspapers do not list a bond's price in terms of its face value. Rather they list it at one-tenth of this value. Thus a bond that sells in the open market at exactly its face value will be said to be trading at 100 instead of $1,000. Similarly, a bond that sells for $800 will be listed as trading at 80, and one that sells for $1,050 will be listed at 105.

Of course, bonds are often traded at fractional prices,

just as stocks are. Usually these fractions consist of one-eighth, one-quarter and one-half points. Thus, if you see that a bond is trading for 98½, you will know that its price in the open market is $985 (98.5 times 10). Again, if it is trading at 98¾, you will know that its price is $987.50 (98.75 times 10).

The major exception to this statement involves United States government bonds, which trade in thirty-seconds of a point. In other words, if a government bond is trading for 70.24, it really means 70²⁴/₃₂. That in turn means 70¾, which is the same as 70.75. This, of course, indicates that the purchaser bought a bond worth $707.50 (70.75 times 10).

A bond is normally issued to sell for its face value, which, as we have seen, is usually $1,000 (100). Thereafter, however, it may sell for more or less. When it sells for more, it is said to be selling at a *premium*. When it sells for less, it is said to be selling at a *discount*.

Nonetheless, not all bonds are issued precisely at their face values. Sometimes they are issued at a slightly higher or lower price. For example, in 1974 some bonds issued by Philadelphia Electric Company were first offered at 100.875. When something like this happens, it usually indicates that the underwriter had to bid more or less than it normally would in order to underwrite the bond issue.

Bonds are almost always issued for a certain length of time or *term*. A few are issued for a term of less than five years. Commonly, however, they are issued for from ten to fifty years, with twenty- and thirty-year bonds being most prevalent.

The expiration of a bond's term represents, of course, its *maturity date,* the date on which its principal amount will be repaid. During the course of its life, a bond may sell for a great deal more or less than its face value. But when it matures, its issuer will pay its owner whatever the face value is.

Chapt 2 (cont)

15,

In actual practice, many bonds are paid off well before they mature. Thus, when a corporation issues a bond, it commonly states right on the bond itself that the bond is subject to *call.* This means that the corporation may redeem the bond in advance of its maturity date.

Usually, however, the bond will not be callable before a certain date. For example, if the bond's term runs for thirty years, the corporation may promise that the bond will not be callable until at least five, or perhaps ten, years of its life have elapsed.

These days, most corporate bonds are callable. Sometimes corporations never exercise this right or only exercise it many years after they are first entitled to do so. Other times they exercise the right as soon as possible.

And when they do, they normally pay a premium over and above the bond's face value. In fact, when a company states that a bond is subject to call, it will stipulate the price it will pay in order to redeem it ahead of its maturity date.

Typically, a call price is equal to a bond's face value, plus its annual interest rate. Thus, if a corporation reserves the right to call in a series of bonds worth $1,000 apiece and paying 8 percent interest, it may promise to pay its bondholders $1,080 for each bond they hold.

At first glance, bonds subject to call may sound like a fine investment. After all, the bondholder will receive more for his bonds than he would if he held them to maturity.

On the other hand, the bondholder will no longer own the bonds nor receive interest on them. If his bonds are called in, he may give up 7 or 8 percent a year in interest and receive a one-time premium that is not likely to be much, if any, larger than that amount.

Furthermore, a company may stipulate that its bonds' call price will steadily decline the longer the bonds remain outstanding. Take some debentures that were issued by American Telephone & Telegraph in May 1974. They pay interest of 8.8 percent and are due to mature in 2005. But they can be called in as early as 1979.

If AT&T redeems them in 1980, it has agreed to pay 107.11 percent of their face value, plus accrued interest. If it waits until 1990 to redeem them, it has agreed to pay 103.72 percent. If it delays until 2000, it has agreed to pay 100.34 percent. Thereafter the call price will equal the face value of the bonds.

Companies usually call in bonds because interest rates have declined sufficiently to compensate them for calling them in early, even though they have to pay a premium to do so. For example, a company may have had to pay interest of 8 percent when it first issued a bond series. But over the course of a few years, the interest commanded by new corporate bonds of its genre may have fallen to 5 or 6 percent. As a result, it may be much cheaper to call in the outstanding bonds and issue new ones at the lower rate of interest.

What determines how much interest a company will have to pay in the first place? Three factors are at work.

The most important is the prevailing rate of interest on bonds of comparable quality. In other words, the organization that issues bonds will have to pay approximately what comparable borrowers have to pay if it hopes to attract any lenders.

This prevailing rate of interest is determined largely by the law of supply and demand. When there is a great deal of demand for money, the interest rate will tend to rise. When demand slackens, the interest rate will probably fall.

Yet this interest rate is also affected by the United States government. Through the Federal Reserve System, the government has considerable control over the amount of money that is pumped into the economy. If the Federal Reserve System increases the amount of money available, it makes it easier to borrow. As a result, the interest rate will tend to fall because supply will catch up with demand. If, however, the Federal Reserve System holds down the supply of new money, the interest rate will tend to rise because demand will probably exceed supply.

Actually, there is no one prevailing rate of interest. There are several rates—both short-term and long-term.

One of the most important of the short-term rates is the federal funds rate, which is the rate that banks charge each other for overnight loans. Another is the prime rate—i.e., the rate banks charge corporate customers of the highest quality. There are also several others of considerable importance, such as the rate on commercial paper.

These short-term rates do not always move in precise conjunction with one another. But they do follow the same broad trend. In other words, they all tend to move upward or downward as the demand for money rises and falls.

Of the long-term rates, one of the most important is the rate on long-term bonds—those that are issued for terms of five years or more. Another is the rate on residential mortgages.

Like short-term rates, long-term rates do not always move in precise conjunction with one another. Yet they also tend to follow the same broad trend.

But this does not mean that short-term rates and long-term rates always move in the same direction. Sometimes they do. And sometimes they don't. Thus, in the early weeks of 1974, short-term rates fell, while long-term rates generally held firm.

Over any extended period of time, however, it is most unlikely that the two sets of rates would move in sharply opposite directions. Both groups are affected too markedly by the law of supply and demand not to respond in somewhat similar fashion.

Since World War II, the trend in the interest rates that corporations have had to pay in order to issue bonds has been ever upward. To be sure, there have been downward tugs and hauls. Even so, in 1945 the most credit-worthy corporations usually did not have to pay more than 2.5 percent to float a bond issue. Before twenty years had passed, they often had to pay 5 percent. And by 1970 the interest rate on bonds of the highest quality had soared well above 9 percent. Since then, the rate has fallen off somewhat, then climbed back up again. As this is written, it is very high by the standards that have prevailed throughout most of this century.

The reasons for the steady increase in interest rates should be obvious. There has been a marked increase in inflation. There has also been an ever-increasing demand for capital on the part of all branches of government, all kinds of corporations and all manner of individuals. The national economy may have suffered recessions and other ups and downs over the past thirty years. But by and large, the nation has enjoyed a high rate of growth and a high level of prosperity.

To sum up then, the going rate of interest on bonds largely determines what any given corporation or governmental body will have to pay to borrow money. Yet the going rate will provide only a ball-park figure. The credit standing of a bond issuer and its ability to continue to prosper will determine the precise amount it will have to pay. If the issuer is well known and well regarded, and if its financial condition is considered sound, it may be able to pay considerably less than another issuer would.

How much less? Perhaps one-quarter of one percentage point. Perhaps one-half of one point. Perhaps a full point. Perhaps more. Although such differences may not sound large, they can add up to millions of dollars in interest payments each and every year.

Whatever interest a bond issuer agrees to pay, it promises to do so for as long as its bond issue is outstanding. Thus, if it agrees to pay 7.5 percent annually, you, the bondholder, will receive $75 a year for each bond you own.

Chpt 2 (cont) 19.

This will be true even if the bond's price fluctuates sharply over the years.

✓ This brings us to another important facet of the bond market—one that is probably discussed much more frequently than interest rates or prices. This facet is known as *current yield* or return.

Important as it is, a bond's current yield is not an entity in and of itself. Rather it reflects the relationship between the price a bond sells at in the open market and its interest rate.

A bond's current yield may be exactly the same as its interest rate. Or it may be more. Or it may be less. Usually it is more or less.

If a bond is issued at its face value of $1,000 (100), if it continues to sell at that price, and if its interest rate is 8 percent, then its yield will also be 8 percent. But if the bond rises in price, its current yield will fall. And if it falls in price, its yield will rise.

This doesn't mean that you won't continue to receive $80 in interest each year. You will. But it does mean that your true rate of return will be more or less than 8 percent, depending on what you paid for the bond.

✓ It's easy to see why when you realize that a bond's current yield is merely determined by dividing its selling price into its interest rate. Thus if you divide a bond whose price is $1,000 into $80, you will obtain a yield of 8 percent. But if you divide a bond whose price is $900 into $80, you will obtain a yield of nearly 8.9 percent. And if you divide a bond whose price is $1,100 into $80, you will obtain a yield of less than 7.3 percent.

✓ This brings up two important principles about bonds. Never forget them.

1) First, a bond's price and its yield always move in opposite directions. They never go up or down together. Inevitably, when one rises, the other falls.

2) Second, it should be obvious that when the prices of

quality bonds fall and their yields rise, it usually has little or nothing to do with the nature of the bonds or with the credit-worthiness of the organizations that issued them. Rather it reflects a rise in interest rates, a rise that tends to affect all bonds more or less impartially.

The prices of old bonds must fall when new ones carry higher interest rates. Otherwise no one would be interested in buying the old ones. So the old ones fall in price sufficiently so that their yields equal or at least approximate those on the new ones.

So far, as you know, we have been talking about *current yield.* But most bond experts believe a bond's *yield to maturity* is much more important.

Yield to maturity includes not only the interest on a bond, but also any profit or loss that will accrue when the bond matures. This profit or loss will represent the difference between the price you paid for the bond and its face value.

Obviously, if you paid less than the face value when you bought the bond, your yield to maturity will be greater than the current yield. But if you paid more than the face value, your yield to maturity will be less than the current yield.

Take an example: a bond that will mature in ten years pays 9 percent interest. It currently sells for $1,100 (110). So its current yield is 8.18 percent ($1,100 into $90). But you will lose $100 of your $1,100 investment when the bond matures. Over a ten-year period, this amounts to a loss of about 1 percent a year. Yet yield to maturity also takes into account compound interest on the difference between purchase price and face value for each year of the bond's life. So the exact yield to maturity will be 7.56 percent.

If, however, you had bought the same $1,000 bond for $900 (90), the situation would be reversed. Then your current yield would be 10 percent ($900 into $90). Furthermore, you would gain $100 when the bond matures. When the interest on this $100 is compounded annually over a ten-year period, it pushes the yield to maturity to 10.65 percent.

But all this will hold true only if the bond is not called in before its maturity date. If it is called in, its yield to call date will be markedly affected. If it was bought at a premium, the yield to call date will be lower than it would be if the bond were allowed to mature. And if the bond was bought at a discount, the yield to call date will be higher.

As you can see, it is easy to figure current yield. It is much more difficult to figure yield to maturity.

Fortunately, there is no need to do so. Most banks, brokerage houses and libraries have standard bond–yield tables that show yields to maturity in accordance with maturity dates, interest rates and so forth. These tables can tell you in a jiffy what the yield to maturity on any given bond will be.

From what has been said so far, you may have assumed that when a corporation wishes to issue bonds, it need only locate an investment banker, agree with him on the terms of the issue, then wait for hungry hordes of investors to make their purchases. Nothing could be further from the truth.

A company that floats a bond issue is seeking a loan. As a result, an investment banker will usually investigate the company with great care before it agrees to underwrite its bonds.

The company may thus find itself in a position not unlike the one you might be in if you were to seek a loan from your local bank. If you are well known and well regarded in your community, and if you have good credit standing, the bank may be willing to lend you $1,000, $5,000 or even more, solely on the basis of your good name. In other words, it won't demand that you put up any collateral as a guarantee that you will repay the loan.

Banks and other investors often take the same attitude toward corporations. The corporations are so big, so well known and so well regarded that, unless some special factor dictates otherwise, they can often issue bonds without putting up collateral. Bonds issued in this fashion carry a special name in common usage in the bond field. They are known as *debentures.*

In recent years, more and more industrial corporations have put out this kind of bond, which now dominates the field by a considerable margin. The reason for the trend is simple: a company's earning power is considered much better protection against the possibility of default than the right to take over its assets.

Whether they issue debentures or bonds requiring some kind of collateral, many companies state in advance that they will pay off some portion of an issue before it matures. To this end, they set aside a fixed number of dollars each year or else some percentage of the total value of the issue. They then use this money to call in some bonds, to purchase them in the open market or to make tenders for them—that is, to ask their owners to turn them in at a certain price. The money that is thus set aside is known as a *sinking fund.*

In 1972 Salomon Brothers, one of the nation's leading bond houses, did a study of nearly 1,000 industrial and finance bonds. The study showed that almost two-thirds of the bonds required use of a sinking fund.*

Thus, in 1974, Anheuser-Busch, General Mills and The Singer Company all issued $100 million worth of sinking fund debentures due to mature in 1999. Obviously all three of the companies will retire some of the bonds before that year.

*See *The Anatomy of the Secondary Market in Corporate Bonds*, Salomon Brothers, New York, 1973.

Singer, for instance, plans to make full use of the money it borrowed until 1980, then retire 5 percent of its debt annually over a twenty-year period. Among its reasons for establishing a sinking fund: the fund provides for orderly retirement of the debt. And it is looked upon with favor by the investment advisory organizations that rate bonds. In other words, these organizations are more apt to give a good rating to a bond with a sinking fund. This means that the issuing corporation will have to pay less interest than would otherwise be the case.

Whether or not they are paid off by means of a sinking fund, other kinds of bonds are backed by collateral. The best known of this group is a *first-mortgage bond.* This kind of bond is secured by all of a company's property, exclusive of its working capital. Sometimes the security includes not only all of the property the company presently owns, but also all the property that it may acquire in the future.

Next comes the *collateral-trust bond,* which is rarely issued these days. When a company does issue a bond of this stripe, it deposits common stock or other assets with a trustee to guarantee payment of principal and interest. Usually the value of these assets exceeds the value of the bonds.

Still other companies issue *income* or *adjustment bonds.* In these instances, a company promises to pay interest on its bonds only if it earns enough to do so. If it doesn't earn enough to pay the full rate, it must pay as much as it can, to the nearest one-half of 1 percent.

For example, it may have promised to pay 7 percent a year only to find that it can pay only one-half of that. So it pays 3.5 percent. The next year, it may pay 2.5 percent or 5.5 percent or the full 7 percent.

Finally, there are so-called *equipment-trust certificates.* These are issued almost exclusively by railroads and other companies in the transportation industry. As you might guess, the money raised by the bonds is used to purchase locomotives or passenger or freight cars or airplanes or ships. The equipment itself serves as collateral for the bonds.

It's worth mentioning that, although they are not referred to as debentures, all bonds issued by the United States government are just that. They are not backed by the White House, the U.S. Capitol Building, the Lincoln Memorial or any other property of the federal government, but only by the government's good faith and authority. The same is true of most bonds issued by states, cities and other local authorities.

The chief exception, as we will see more fully in Chapter 7, involves municipal bonds backed by a tax or other specific source of income. Even then, however, the bondholder has no right to seize a bridge or a housing project should the issuer default. In other words, the lower level governmental bodies do not put up collateral as that term is commonly thought of.

In essence, then, there are basically only two kinds of bonds: debentures, which are backed only by a company's general reputation and credit standing, and all other kinds of bonds, which are backed by some kind of collateral or, as in the case of income bonds, by some specific promise to pay.

It may seem as if first-mortgage bonds were the safest of all bonds. Nonetheless, debentures often make as good an, if not a better, investment. In other words, the nature of the issuing company rather than the nature of its bonds really governs the bonds' safety.

In addition to bonds, corporations, governments and other public bodies sometimes issue *notes*. Indeed, in 1973 at least, municipalities issued notes with a greater total face value than that of the bonds they put out.

In many ways, notes are just like bonds. Thus they have a face value, return a stated rate of interest, mature at a specific date in the future, and can be bought and sold on the open market.

The chief difference is that notes are often issued for a term of no more than seven years—and frequently for much shorter periods. Bonds, on the other hand, are usually issued for much longer periods.

Organizations sometimes prefer to issue notes rather than bonds because they do not want to commit themselves to pay high rates of interest over a long period of time. They hope that, when the notes mature, interest rates will have fallen.

Interestingly, a few organizations recently came to grips with this problem in a novel way. In the summer of 1974, a number of nationally prominent bank-holding companies, plus at least two huge industrial corporations, issued so-called *floating-rate notes*. These notes, which are similar but not necessarily identical, will carry a fixed rate of interest for a number of months. Then they will return interest that in most cases will be one percent higher than the rate on U.S. Treasury bills that mature in three months.

The latter rate, which is considered a good barometer of interest rates, fluctuates frequently and often sharply. For example, it was well under 4 percent during certain periods of 1967, 1971 and 1972. But it ran in excess of 9 percent during part of 1974.

If you are to understand bonds fully, there are two other terms you should know: *bearer bonds* and *registered bonds*.

There was a time when bearer bonds were far and away the most common kind of bond. These bonds usually had coupons attached to them, and the owner merely clipped the coupons off every few months and mailed or took them to his bank, to the issuing corporation or to its paying agent. He was then presented with the interest that was due him.

It was long believed that bearer bonds were easily transferable. This was and still is true. As their very name implies, these bonds are assumed to belong to whoever bears or possesses them. But as you can guess, they are subject to loss through fire or theft.

And, among corporations at least, they are gradually passing from favor. Most corporations now register the names of their bonds' owners on their books and on the bonds themselves. They then mail interest to the owners as it falls due, usually every six months.

If you should buy a bond, then sell it, you will be entitled to whatever amount of interest has built up since the last interest-payment date. For example, if you own a bond that pays 8 percent in interest and you sell it three months to the day after the previous interest payment, you will obtain 2 percent in interest—equal, of course, to one-quarter of the total interest due for the year. This kind of interest is known as *accrued interest*. And it is paid by a bond's buyer.

As of a recent date, nearly 2,000 bonds were listed on the New York Stock Exchange. Nearly 200 more were listed on the American Stock Exchange. Still others were listed on various regional exchanges, such as the Pacific Stock Exchange. Yet these bonds represent only a small portion of the total. The overwhelming majority of bonds are traded in the over-the-counter market.

This market, as you know if you have ever bought or sold stocks, is not a central market with its own building, organization, staff and so forth. Rather it consists of hundreds of dealers around the country who are linked only by telephone or more recently by the National Association of Securities Dealers Automated Quotation (NASDQ).

The reasons most bonds are traded only in the over-the-counter market are quite simple. For one thing, it's much cheaper. Corporations can sometimes avoid hundreds of thousands of dollars in filing fees by not listing their bonds on an exchange. For another thing, it cuts red tape. Finally, unless a corporation is deliberately seeking a sizable number of individual investors, there is no particular advantage to being traded on an exchange. Institutional investors are not apt to be impressed with the prestige that supposedly accrues from an exchange listing.

All this means, however, that you cannot always pick up your morning newspaper and learn what a particular bond is selling for. To find that out, you will have to call or write your broker.

Yet this is not so inconvenient as it may sound. That's because most individual investors do not buy bonds with the thought of selling them in a year or two, but with the thought of holding onto them for many years, perhaps until they mature.

Even so, bonds are sold from time to time, in much the same fashion stocks are. We will examine the details in Chapter 10.

What are the most important facts we have learned in this chapter? Four stand out.

A bond is, in effect, a loan to a corporation, government or other public body. The bond itself stands as the issuer's promise to pay back the loan on a certain date in the future and in the meantime to pay a guaranteed rate of interest that is fixed for the life of the bond. The amount of interest that is payable will be determined in part by the size of the demand to borrow money at any given point in time and in part by the credit standing and earning power of the issuer. More important than the bond's interest rate is its yield, which reflects the real rate of return on the buyer's investment. Finally, bonds are backed either by the credit standing of the issuer or by some specific collateral and are traded in much the same way stocks are, although usually in the over-the-counter market.

You can go a long way toward determining whether you

have mastered the other information in this chapter by
seeing if you can decipher the following bond listing, which
is reproduced exactly as it appeared in a recent issue of *The
New York Times:*

ATT 8¾ 2000 8.1 243 107 106⅝ 107 +⅛

Not sure of every figure? Here is the explanation:

The bonds were issued by American Telephone & Telegraph and pay interest of 8.75 percent a year. They will
mature in the year 2000. At the time in question, they had
a current yield of 8.1 percent. On the day preceding the
newspaper listing, $243,000 worth of the bonds was
traded. The highest price at which they traded was 107
($1,070). The lowest price was 106⅝. The highest price
was also the final price. This represented a gain of one-
eighth of a point over the final price on the last previous
day on which they were traded.

So much for the ABC's of bonds.

End of chpt. 2

Chapter 3

How Bonds Are Rated

If you invest in common stocks, you probably do so with
the help of a broker. If you use him regularly, he undoubtedly sends you various research reports published by his
brokerage house. As you know, these reports discuss the
merits of buying, selling or holding onto various stocks and
usually devote anywhere from 25 to 2,500 words to detail-
ing each recommendation.

If you ever invest in bonds, it's unlikely that you will
receive such comprehensive reports. Although they exist,
most brokerage houses provide their clients with much
sparser information.

For example, one report that recently crossed my desk
listed fifteen corporate bonds. The report included only
the following information about each bond: the name of
the issuing company, the interest payable on the bond, the

date it will mature, its rating, its price, its current yield, its yield to maturity, its call features—that is, when it may be called in and at what price—and its amount outstanding.

Of all such information, none is more important than a bond's rating. This rating is designed to inform all investors, institutional and individual alike, of one thing and one thing only: how likely it is that the issuing company will be able to repay the money it has borrowed, plus interest along the way, and do both of these things on time.

Three organizations in this country rate corporate and municipal bonds and notes. The three organizations are, alphabetically, Fitch Investors Service Incorporated, Moody's Investor Service Incorporated and Standard & Poor's Corporation. The last two organizations are far more important than the first. Their ratings are more widely publicized, referred to and depended upon.

Just what are the ratings they issue, and what do these ratings signify? Standard & Poor's rates all bonds on a scale stretching from triple-A (AAA) through single-D (D). The significance of its ratings is as follows:

- AAA——Bonds with this rating are considered obligations of the highest grade. They provide the ultimate degree of protection for both principal and interest. And their prices move up and down only as interest rates move up and down.

- AA——Bonds with this rating also qualify as high-grade obligations and differ from AAA bonds only in small degree. Their prices also move in conjunction with interest rates.

- A——Bonds with this rating are regarded as upper medium grade. Their principal and interest are safe, and they have considerable investment strength. But their prices reflect not only changes in interest rates but also, to some extent, changes in economic and trade conditions.

- BBB——Bonds with this rating are considered medium grade. They have adequate asset coverage and are normally protected by satisfactory earnings. But their prices respond more to business conditions than to interest rates, and they need constant watching. In short, these bonds fall between definitely sound obligations and obligations dominated by a speculative element, and are the lowest grade of bond qualifying for investment by most institutions.

- BB——Bonds with this rating are regarded as lower medium grade. The fortunes of the companies that issue them may change swiftly as economic conditions change. Utility bonds in this category consistently earn interest by narrow margins. Other kinds of bonds earn interest by fair margins. Yet during economic downturns, deficit operations are possible.

- B——Bonds with this rating are regarded as speculative. When difficult economic conditions prevail, interest rates cannot be assured.

- CCC——Bonds with this rating are regarded as extremely speculative. Their issuers pay interest, but it is questionable whether they will do so if trade conditions become poor.

- CC——Bonds with this rating are more speculative yet. Their issuers may have agreed to pay interest only when they earn income. And under any conditions, payments may be small.

- C——Bonds with this rating meet two clear-cut criteria: their issuers have agreed to pay interest only when

they earn income; and they are presently doing neither.

- DDD, DD and D——Bonds with these ratings are in
default on payments of principal, payments of interest
or both. The particular rating indicates a bond's salvage value in relation to other bonds' salvage values.

If you have studied these ratings carefully, you will have
noticed that the great dividing line involves bonds rated
BBB. All bonds with higher ratings are considered safe
investments for both institutions and individuals. All bonds
with lower ratings are considered at least slightly unsafe.
There is a strong speculative element to them and, unless
you are an experienced investor who knows what he is
doing, most investment counselors would advise you not to
invest in them.

What about the bonds right on the dividing line—those
with BBB ratings? There, you will get an argument. Some
investment counselors would advise sticking only to bonds
rated A or better. Others would say that, if you use ordinary
prudence, you can find plenty of bonds rated BBB that
constitute good investments.

By the same token, some institutions limit their investments to bonds rated AAA, AA or A. Others limit them to
those three groups, plus the BBB group.

Both approaches are sound. Much depends on the nature and requirements of the investor. The more important
it is that he have virtually an absolute guarantee that he will
receive payment of principal, plus interest, the more apt he
will be to stick to bonds rated A or better.

In short, BBB bonds are the first to contain a speculative
element. Those with lower ratings are clearly speculative to
one degree or another. Naturally, they also pay higher rates
of interest. But there is some question whether their issuers
will always be able to pay this interest.

Recently, Standard & Poor's has begun adding plus and minus signs to some of its ratings. Thus a bond may be rated A+ or BBB−.

The addition of these symbols is designed to indicate the relative credit standing of the bonds in question. For example, bonds rated A+ are deemed to be slightly superior to other bonds with A ratings.

The plus symbol is used to define both new and seasoned issues, when appropriate. The minus symbol is used only in relation to seasoned issues and, when applied, it indicates that the credit standing of the bond issuer is deteriorating. Neither symbol is applied to bonds rated AAA or those rated lower than BB.

Fitch employs exactly the same rating symbols as Standard & Poor's, without the plus and minus signs. Moody's employs slightly different ones.

Thus, when Moody's wants to give a bond the highest possible rating, it gives it an Aaa instead of an AAA. When it wants to give it the second highest possible rating, it gives it an Aa instead of an AA.

And so on down the line. Thus its Baa equals the BBB given by Fitch and Standard & Poor's. And its Ba equals the BB given by the latter two organizations.

Through the first six ratings—that is, from AAA through B—the meaning of the symbols employed by Moody's and Standard & Poor's are the same. Thus, when Moody's rates a bond Aaa and Standard & Poor's rates it AAA, they have identical or virtually identical opinions of it.

Moody's, however, does not issue any ratings lower than C. So some bonds to which it gives ratings of Caa, Ca or C may be in default. Standard & Poor's ordinarily gives bonds in default a rating of DDD or less.

Although the two top rating organizations usually agree on the meaning of the ratings they employ, they do not always agree on how a given bond should be rated. H.

Russell Fraser, vice president of Standard & Poor's corporate finance department, estimates that the two organizations differ on one in every five bonds issued by utility companies and one in every ten issued by industrial companies.

Nonetheless, the ratings made by the two investment advisory organizations rarely, if ever, differ by more than one grade. Thus Moody's may rate a bond Aaa, while Standard & Poor's rates it only AA. But it would be most unlikely, if not unheard of, for the two organizations to differ more strongly than that.

The reason their ratings are usually the same and almost never more than one grade apart should be obvious. They both have access to the same statistics. These statistics tell a great deal about the issuer's ability to repay the principal it plans to borrow, plus interest along the way.

The reason that the two organizations sometimes differ is that rating bonds is an art, not a science. As Fraser puts it: "If we used only figures—a company's sales and earnings records, its ratio of assets to debt and so forth—we could tell you the rating its bond should get within ten minutes. But figures don't tell the whole story about a company or, sometimes, even the true story.

"So we must supplement figures with other facts. What new products is the company planning to bring out? What are its research goals? What are its acquisition plans? What is the likely future of its industry?

"We can get facts like these only from top management. Once we have them, it may take ten hours rather than ten minutes to decide how to rate the bond."

Obviously, the rating a bond receives is very important to the investor. It tells him whether it is almost certain, highly probable or merely possible that he will get his investment back and be paid interest on that investment when he is supposed to be.

Yet this rating is every bit as important to the company or municipality that issues the bond. For the rating goes a long way toward determining how much interest the issuer will have to pay. The lower the rating, the more interest investors will want.

Take the early months of 1974. An industrial company whose bond received a rating of AAA would probably have had to pay interest of 7.75 percent, presuming the bond couldn't be called in for at least five years. But if the bond had been rated BBB, the company would have had to pay interest of perhaps 9.25 percent.

If the firm had been seeking $10 million, repayable in thirty years, the difference in the two ratings would have cost it $4.5 million in extra interest over the life of the bond. If it had been seeking $100 million, the difference would have cost it a whopping $45 million.

What's more, when a bond receives a low rating, a company may not be able to bring it to market at all. There simply may not be enough investor interest in it.

For example, in 1970 the Pennsylvania Company, the holding company for the Penn Central Railroad, wanted to sell $100 million worth of debentures due to mature in 1994. It was willing to pay interest of better than 11 percent.

But before the bonds were brought to market, Standard & Poor's rated them BB. For that and other reasons, they failed to elicit interest, and the Pennsylvania Company never actually brought them out.

Even when a company can sell a low-rated bond, the rating will be a blow to its pride and perhaps its prestige, thus affecting all its efforts to raise money from other sources. Furthermore, the company's underwriting syndicate will have to absorb the loss on any portion that is not sold, making it less likely that it will want to do business with the company in the future.

36 HOW TO INVEST IN BONDS

Before examining how the investment advisory organizations make their ratings, there are several other facets of bond-rating that you should understand.

First, the overwhelming majority of corporate bonds receive a rating of A or better. Thus the 1972 study done by Salomon Brothers shows that of nearly 3,900 issues rated by Standard & Poor's, more than 83 percent were rated AAA, AA or A. About another 10 percent were rated BBB.

Does it surprise you that the vast proportion of bonds receive high ratings? It shouldn't. Remember, we are not talking about a company's ability to become the biggest and most important firm in its industry, to open up sizable new markets, or to treble or quadruple its earnings in a short period of time. We are talking about its ability to pay back what it borrows, with interest, and to do so on schedule.

A company that cannot pay interest on schedule is in trouble. A company that cannot pay back principal on schedule is in big trouble. Indeed, it is in danger of going bankrupt.

You should also understand that bond ratings are not necessarily forever. They can be and sometimes are changed.

When a change takes place, it does not affect the amount of interest that the issuing organization must pay on the bonds it already has outstanding. But it may affect the prices of those bonds in the marketplace. And it will almost certainly affect the amount of interest that the company will have to pay on future issues.

Standard & Poor's reviews all its ratings annually. In a typical year, says Russell Fraser, it changes its ratings on about one in every twenty corporate issues and one in every twenty-five municipal issues.

The ratings may go up or down. And for all one can tell,

within another few years, they may be changed back again.

For example, in 1965 Moody's slashed its rating on bonds issued by the City of New York from A to Baa. A year later, Standard & Poor's followed suit. A major reason: the city was selling bonds to pay for current operating expenses rather than for capital expenditures.

The downgrading brought cries of outrage from Mayor Abraham D. Beame, then the city's controller. He even called for federal regulation of the investment advisory organizations. But, of course, he got nowhere.

In 1972, however, Moody's pushed the city's rating back up to A. A year later, Standard & Poor's again followed suit, leading Beame to assert that it was only a first step toward a still higher rating.

Why the change in heart by the investment advisory organizations? There were many reasons. Among others, the city had consistently been able to overcome financial difficulties and seemed in a stronger position than it had been a few years earlier.

A few months after Standard & Poor's issued its new rating, the city brought out $362 million worth of short-term notes. Partly as a result of the change in rating, it saved some $2.1 million in interest over what it would have had to pay if the rating had remained the same.

Another thing you should understand is that convertible bonds rarely obtain ratings of A or better. In fact, the majority of convertible bonds are rated BB or lower.

There are several reasons why. As we will see more fully in Chapter 6, convertible bonds are often made convertible because they would not be particularly attractive to investors if issued as straight bonds. Then too, by their very nature, they are much more volatile than straight bonds. Their prices tend to fluctuate more frequently, rapidly and widely.

You should also be aware that the three investment

advisory organizations do not necessarily rate all bonds. Standard & Poor's, for example, does not rate bonds issued by banks. Fraser explains that banks constitute a unique, closely regulated business and that they have to be more careful of their reputations than most. As a result, there is less need to rate their bonds.

Neither does Standard & Poor's rate the issues put out by the U.S. Treasury or various government agencies. It reasons that these are the safest of all bonds and, therefore, that other bonds should be rated in relation to them.*

Standard & Poor's doesn't rate bonds issued by real estate investment trusts either. It thinks most of the trusts haven't been in business long enough to be judged.

Finally, the investment advisory organization does not rate bonds brought out by corporations that cannot provide audited financial statements. Or those that do not have demonstrable operating records. Or those that are not seeking at least $5 million.

But these are all exceptions. Moody's and Standard & Poor's do rate the overwhelming majority of publicly issued corporate and municipal issues. But unless asked to do so, they do not rate privately placed issues.

You should also understand that the two big investment advisory organizations rate corporate and municipal notes as well as bonds. These notes are given the same kind of ratings the bonds are.

To make their ratings, the two organizations have a sizable number of security analysts, plus supporting personnel. At Standard & Poor's two analysts are normally assigned to make a single rating. They report their recommendations to three other analysts, and the five of them vote on what the rating should be.

---

*Moody's does rate many, although far from all, Treasury and government agency issues. Specifically, it rates those that are issued directly by the Treasury or that are fully guaranteed by the government. Always or almost always, it gives these issues a rating of triple-A.

Usually, majority rule prevails. But when it is proposed that a bond's rating be changed, the vote must be unanimous or almost so.

How do the analysts go about rating corporate bonds? They are almost exclusively interested in four facets of any given bond. In ascending order of importance, these facets are the bond's indenture provisions, the property protection behind it (that is, how heavily encumbered the company is by other debt), the company's financial resources and its future earning power.

Obviously, the analysts spend a great deal of time studying published reports about the company in question. For example, they pore over its recent annual and interim reports, the bond registration form it has filed with the Securities & Exchange Commission, plus historical information from the rating agency's own library. On occasion, they may also telephone the company's competitors or other trade sources.

But more and more, they want to talk with the management of the issuing company. A decade ago, the investment advisory organization met with representatives of only a few dozen corporations each year. In 1973 it met with the representatives of 1,200.

Explains Fraser: "Many more bonds are being issued than once was the case. The pace of business is quickening very rapidly. And business conditions seem to be changing more often. One day, you don't have an energy crisis. The next day, you have one that seems likely to affect business for years to come. In order to keep on top of things, we must meet face to face with management."

Even so, the analysts begin their study with the indenture, which is a legal document that spells out the restrictions under which a company must operate once it has issued a bond. Thus the indenture includes a promise to pay principal and interest at certain stated times, indicates what will happen if the company defaults on either, tells where and how the bonds may be transferred and exchanged, and lists the conditions under which the company may consolidate its operations or merge with another company.

In studying indenture provisions, bond raters are really interested in just six questions:

- Do the provisions deviate from standard practice? If so, why?

- Is the indenture too restrictive? For example, is it apt to deter a company from acquisitions or expansions that may become necessary in the future?

- Does it allow the company to issue other bonds that would have an equal or greater claim on the company's assets than the bond in question? Standard & Poor's ordinarily prefers that future bond issues be made subordinate. It also prefers that there be a reasonable limit on the amount of additional debt that can be issued.

- Does it spell out standards the company must meet before it can issue other bonds? Normally, the investment advisory organization prefers that an industrial company's adjusted net tangible assets be at least two and one-half times as big as its current and proposed debt. Its net tangible assets are equal to the net value of its plant, plus the value of all its other tangible assets, plus its working capital, less all deferred charges and all reserves it has set aside against liabilities.

- Does the indenture require establishment of a sinking fund? In the case of an electric utility, the rating organization may be satisfied with a property fund, into which the utility will put money with which to improve its plant. In the case of an industrial firm, it doesn't insist upon, but does prefer, a cash sinking fund. Normally, it likes the issuer to retire at least 75 percent of the bond's principal by the time the bond matures.

• If there is a lien on the company's property, is it specific? These days industrial bonds usually don't carry liens. But utility bonds sometimes do. When this is the case, Standard & Poor's wants to be sure that the lien grants the lender control of all property, including franchises and property rights, in case of default. To gain control of a telephone utility without controlling its franchises, Fraser points out, would be an exercise in futility.

Indenture provisions can be important. Some evidence: in 1973, Georgia Power had to postpone a public offering of bonds and preferred stock because it wasn't earning enough to cover interest payments two times over, as its indenture required.

In studying a company's property protection, Standard & Poor's is really interested in only two questions: how heavily is the company already encumbered by debt? What is its debt-retirement policy?

To answer the first question, Standard & Poor's studies several ratios. The most important, as we have already seen, is the ratio of net tangible assets to debt. The rating organization usually insists that this ratio be at least two and one-half to one. And it prefers that it be three and one-half to one.

United States Steel learned just how important property protection is in 1970, when Standard & Poor's reviewed the AA rating on its bonds. The company had just emerged from a rocky decade. Its long-term debt had increased almost threefold. Its assets-to-debt ratio had dipped below the minimum preferred by Standard & Poor's. Its earnings had been very erratic. And the price of its stock had slumped more than two-thirds.

But two factors were in its favor. The decade had been one of planned refurbishment. More important, the raw materials on its balance sheet were grossly undervalued. It actually had enough supplies on hand to operate for forty years. As a result, it kept its AA rating, but then lost it a few years later because of declining earnings.

A sinking fund is one indication of a sound debt-retirement policy. Such a fund is especially important in the case of companies in extractive industries like copper, gas and oil. That's because their properties only have value as they are put to use. If the companies defaulted, their bondholders might recover little of immediate worth.

As a result, Standard & Poor's often likes companies in the extractive industries to make full payouts of principal, as opposed to 75 percent payouts, before their bonds mature. It may also seek to restrict the lives of the bonds to twenty years instead of thirty.

In studying a company's financial resources, Standard & Poor's wants to know how much cash and working capital the company has. This figure will provide some indication of how capable the company is of riding out a recession without defaulting on interest or sinking fund payments. The figure will also provide some indication of how capable the company is of financing improvements or expanding its sales volume without resort to further borrowing.

Standard & Poor's wants to know: how much cash does the company generate by its own efforts? Have its total cash resources recently been reduced? How big are its bank loans? How long have they been outstanding? Has the company historically been too dependent on banks? As Fraser puts it: "We are interested not just in the size of a company's financial resources, but also in their character."

The investment advisory organization also studies the company's dividend policies. It's wary of a company that regularly makes overly liberal payments to its stockholders. Such payments may indicate that it isn't doing enough to protect itself against a rainy day.

There is no nationwide benchmark as to what constitutes reasonable, but not excessive, dividend payments. Policies often vary sharply from industry to industry. So Standard & Poor's compares the policies of the issuing company with those of its direct competitors.

A company's future earning power is more important than these first three factors put together. As Fraser explains: "Today cash flow is the name of the game."

To ascertain future earning power, Standard & Poor's analysts first pore through the written material they have. They want to know the nature of the industry the company is in, whether it is a growth industry or a mature industry, and whether demand for its products is stable or cyclical. They also want to know the company's past record, in particular whether it has increased its share of its market or at least its sales and earnings, and whether it has reduced some of its cash ratios.

In addition, they want to know the company's depreciation practices and whether these practices are in line with those of other companies in its industry. If the company doesn't set aside enough toward depreciation, it may be inflating its earnings.

Finally, they want to know the company's tax practices. Whether a company charges off investment credits in the year they are realized or spreads them over a period of years has a direct influence on its earnings.

All this information gives the analysts a good fix on the company's past. But the past is important only as it sheds light on the future. To learn more about this future, the analysts usually want to talk with management.

In fact, they want to obtain insight into management itself. As Fraser puts it: "We are concerned with the philosophy, experience, maturity, capability and depth of management. If management turnover is excessive and the company frequently has to go outside its own ranks for new executives, it usually indicates something is wrong.

"How fast is management on its feet? What is the biggest single problem it faces? What is the greatest challenge? Where is it trying to take the company? How will it get there? And how long will it take? We are almost certain to ask all of these questions."

The analysts also probe several other areas. Among them:

- How much is the company spending on research and development? Ordinarily, the analysts are concerned if a company is spending a considerably smaller amount, relative to its sales, than the leaders in its industry.

- What are its new product plans? One way to assess the efficacy of these plans is to check the company's new product record in the recent past.

- What are its other plans for the immediate future? "Management sometimes makes glowing predictions of what its company will be like in four or five years," observes Fraser. "But you can sometimes get a better line on a company by asking what it will be like twelve months hence."

- What are its acquisition plans, if any? The analysts have no bias against acquisitions. But they are aware that many companies got into trouble a few years ago by seeming to make acquisitions for acquisition's sake and by entering fields they knew nothing about. Not surprisingly, Fraser says widely diversified companies are the hardest to rate.

- What methods of financial control does the company employ? "You'd be amazed at the number of companies that don't conduct internal audits," says Fraser. "The absence of such audits can lead to unhappy surprises."

This, then, is how Standard & Poor's goes about rating a corporate bond. As you can see, it is no easy job. It requires evaluation of many factors, some of them of a subjective nature.

Yet, as we have seen, most companies fare reasonably well. A few years ago, for instance, Standard & Poor's studied a bond issue about to be put out by General Foods. Here's how the company looked to the investment advisory organization at that time:

It was in a consistent, noncyclical industry. It was one of the leaders in that industry. It was well dispersed geographically, and it marketed products that had wide consumer appeal. Its earnings had increased each year for eighteen straight years. Its cash flow was equal to almost two-thirds of its debt, and its working capital exceeded its debt by about a five-to-three margin. Result: the bond issue got a rating of AAA.

In 1974 General Foods again plunged into the long-term debt market, bringing out $100 million worth of fourteen-year notes. It still looked good to Standard & Poor's, and its notes were also given a rating of AAA.

In studying municipal bonds, which are put out by states, cities and various public authorities, Standard & Poor's looks at many of the same factors it looks at in studying corporate bonds. Obviously, however, there are important differences between the two kinds of bonds.

In fact, it is probably more difficult to rate a municipal than a corporate bond. That's because there are more intangibles involved.

As Fraser explains: "There are no sales and earnings figures to look at, no profit-and-loss statements, no return-on-capital ratios. Furthermore, there are no competitive factors to assess. The State of Maine and the State of Washington may want to bring bond issues to market at the same time. But aside from this, they do not compete with each other in the sense that General Motors competes with Ford."

So Standard & Poor's has to look at other factors: what are the needs of the state or city that is issuing the bond? What is its debt per capita? What is the ratio of its tax-supported debt to the assessed valuation of its real estate? How adequate is its budget? How big a burden is that budget on taxpayers? What is the area's outlook for industrial growth? Its outlook for population growth?

For reasons that will become clear in Chapter 7, municipal bonds are considered among the safest of all bonds. Nonetheless, not all municipal bonds get top ratings.

For instance, in 1974 the New Jersey Sports and Exposition Authority issued $302 million worth of bonds. The proceeds will be used to finance the construction of a huge sports complex in the Hackensack Meadowlands. The complex will include a race track and a 75,000-seat stadium for the professional football team presently known as the New York Giants. Revenue from the complex is expected to pay for the bonds.

But the Authority had to agree to pay interest of 7.5 percent in order to sell the bonds. This is an unusually high rate of interest to pay on a municipal bond.

Furthermore, the investment advisory organizations were not overly impressed with the bonds' other terms, and Standard & Poor's rated the issue BBB. A major reason: if the complex doesn't generate enough revenue to pay off the bond's principal and interest, the New Jersey state legislature has made a mere moral commitment to step into the breach.

"A moral commitment," observes Fraser, "is hardly a legal guarantee. Administrations and legislatures change. Today's promise could conceivably go unhonored ten years down the road."

This, then, should give you a good idea of how investment advisory organizations go about rating bonds. Actually, you have probably learned more than you need to know.

The significant facts to remember are these: three investment advisory organizations rate bonds on a scale ranging from AAA through D, although Moody's does not issue any ratings lower than C. Most bonds receive ratings of AAA, AA or A and are considered safe investments. Many bonds with BBB ratings are also considered reasonably safe. Those with lower ratings contain a considerable speculative element. The lower the rating, of course, the more interest the issuer will usually have to pay. But ratings can be upgraded or downgraded. And when a rating is lowered, it may bring about a drop in the bond's price, although it will not affect the amount of interest that must be paid on the bond but rather the amount that will have to be paid on future bonds issued by the same organization.

You can, of course, go beyond the ratings. You can do your own research by studying annual reports, balance sheets and the like. If you become deeply involved in bonds, such research may prove wise. If you are a typical investor, however, further research will probably be a waste of time. You are unlikely to uncover anything that the rating agencies don't already know or haven't already considered.

Nor is your interpretation of the factors that affect a

bond likely to contain a greater amount of healthy skepticism. As Fraser puts it: "Our responsibility is not to the corporation or municipality that issues a bond, but to the institution or individual who may consider buying it."

All this doesn't mean the rating agencies do a perfect job. Indeed, in 1974 the Twentieth Century Fund, a research organization, issued an impressive, low-key critique of municipal bond ratings.* Among other things, the fund took the agencies to task for not explaining more clearly what their ratings mean and precisely what they measure. Even so, the fund praised the agencies for doing a "creditable" and ever-improving job.

*See *The Rating Game*, The Twentieth Century Fund, New York, 1974.

Chapter 4

Why Buy Bonds?

Why invest in bonds? Why, for that matter, invest in anything? Obviously, because you hope to make money. Because you think you will do better to invest what you have than to stuff it in a cardboard box or hide it under a mattress.

Yet there are people who should probably not invest at all. And there are other people who probably should not invest in bonds. How can you tell if you belong in one or the other of these two categories?

I suppose that every basic brochure on investments ever published has stressed that before anyone considers investing he should make sure he has enough money to cover basic living expenses, plus some luxuries. In addition, such brochures usually emphasize that the investor should have adequate insurance, plus enough ready cash to meet major and minor emergencies. In short, he should have a good-sized savings account.

But why not leave all excess funds in a savings account? Plenty of people do. And these days they have some justification. As this is written, many banks across the country are paying 7.5 percent interest each year on accounts containing at least $1,000. When this interest is compounded, the total return works out to 7.9 percent.

Unfortunately, the money has to be left in such an account for at least four years. If it is withdrawn earlier, the depositor must pay a penalty that will reduce his yield considerably. Furthermore, there is no guarantee that banks will always pay this rate of interest. Finally, certain other investments may offer even bigger yields. Bonds are a notable case in point.

This is partly because the federal government has put a limit on the interest rates that can be paid on certain of its own debt issues and by commercial banks, savings banks, and savings and loan associations. It is argued that if the government and the thrift institutions paid the going rate of interest, people might pull their money out of some investment vehicles and put them into others.

For example, if the government paid 8 percent interest on its savings bonds, people would withdraw their savings from savings and loan associations. As a result, these associations would not have enough money to lend people for mortgages on their homes.

Then there is the decades-old problem of inflation. It has been with us for as long as many of us can remember, and recently it has become worse. As this is written, no pronounced relief is in sight.

Even a savings account that returns 7.9 percent annually cannot match this rate of inflation. And, of course, the typical savings account does not return 7.9 percent. It is more apt to return 5 or 5.25 or 6 percent.

What's more, savings accounts offer absolutely no chance of achieving capital gains. So, in recent years at least, the person who has kept all his money in a savings account has lost ground to inflation.

All this is a long way of saying that although everyone should keep some money in a savings account, he is well advised to invest funds above and beyond what he needs for a rainy day. To what end? As already suggested, to the making of more money.

Yet this simple answer is a little too simple. Historically, when people have invested money, they have tried to fulfill one or more of three basic purposes. These purposes are known as safety of principal, liberal income and capital appreciation.

Safety of principal means just what its name implies. Above all else, the investor wants to be sure that he will get his investment back at some specific date in the future. Perhaps he wants it back in order to educate his children. Perhaps he wants it back in order to establish an estate for his wife and family. Perhaps he has some other end in mind. Whatever his aim, when he invests his money, he wants to take the least possible risk with it.

Liberal income also means what its name implies. The investor wants to obtain a very good return on his investment, a return equal to or in excess of the going rate. He cannot or does not want to depend solely on salary, fees or other earnings to pay his living expenses. Perhaps the investor is retired or for other reasons receives little or nothing in the way of regular income beyond pension or Social Security payments. Whatever his situation, he wants to supplement his regular income with income from an investment.

By definition, capital appreciation implies growth in the value of an investment. The investor may care little about safety of principal. He may be willing to risk the loss of his entire investment in the expectation that he will not lose it but rather watch its value increase twofold or fivefold or even one hundredfold within the space of a few months or many years. He may also care little about receiving income from his investment. Instead he seeks to make his investment grow. He may need more money in order to buy a house, to educate his children, to travel abroad or to build an estate for his wife and family. Whatever his exact purpose, he seeks big gains in the value of his holdings.

These three goals are not necessarily mutually exclusive. In fact, it's rather easy to make an investment that promises considerable safety of principal and liberal income. It is almost as easy to make an investment that promises liberal income, plus some chance of capital appreciation.

But, although it may be easy to fulfill two of these goals at once, it is not so easy to fulfill all three. Even when an investor can do so, he will not be able to fulfill each goal to the degree he could if he concentrated on just one or two of them. He will not able to achieve maximum safety of principal, maximum liberal income and maximum opportunity for capital appreciation all at the same time. In other words, it is best to make one goal one's primary end, another one's secondary end and recognize that, by definition, there will be considerable constraint on achieving the third.

Now how do bonds stack up against these three goals? Generalizations, of course, are almost always dangerous. There are always exceptions.

Yet it is an unspoken assumption of the investment world that bonds usually provide a great deal of safety of principal. Indeed, as a rule, there is probably no safer investment, presuming the investor can wait until his bonds mature and does not have to sell them earlier for what could be less than their face value.

Bonds also tend to provide liberal income. They usually yield more than preferred stocks. They also usually yield more than common stocks—certainly more than most growth stocks.

Even when the yields on bonds are little or no higher than those on preferred or common stocks, they are regarded as steadier and more certain. As we have already seen, a company must always pay interest to its bondholders before it pays a penny in dividends to its preferred or common stockholders. And even should a company pay a liberal dividend to its stockholders, it may slash this dividend or eliminate it altogether a few years down the road. It cannot, of course, slash or eliminate the interest it pays its bondholders.

On the other hand, bonds usually offer little chance for capital appreciation. As Frank P. Wendt, president of John Nuveen & Co., a nationally known dealer in municipal bonds, announced not long ago to the New York Society of Security Analysts: "There have been very few occasions during my twenty-six years in the business that the bond markets have provided spectacular profit opportunities. That simply is not the nature of our business."

Naturally, you may buy a bond that is selling well below its face value—for, say, $600 or $700 instead of the $1,000 it will be worth when it matures. If you hold the bond until maturity, you will reap a respectable capital gain. Yet if this capital gain is divided by the number of years you must wait until the bond matures, it will not usually seem quite so big.

As we will see more fully in a moment, you can also speculate in bonds, just as you can in stocks or commodities. Speculation has been part of the bond market for as long as that market has been in existence. It will continue to be part of the market for as long as we can foresee.

But to mention speculation is to beg the main point—namely, that bonds are not normally thought of as a way to enlarge capital. Rather they are thought of as a way to preserve capital and to obtain a good income from it.

Of course, if you invest in bonds that pay interest of 8 percent a year, you will double your money in about nine years, assuming you reinvest the interest. If you invest in bonds that pay interest of 9 percent a year, you will double your money in about eight years. And obviously, you will achieve a return greater than the average return on stocks of 8.5 percent cited in Chapter 1.

But again you will beg the main point. For, if you invest in bonds that return 8 or 9 percent a year, you will give up the chance to invest in stocks that may appreciate at a much faster rate than 8.5 percent a year. You will take a safe capital gain and give up the chance to make a sensational one.

To reiterate, most people invest in bonds not to make capital gains, but to preserve their capital and get a good return from it. Should that also be your goal?

In investing it is important that you do not establish goals that cannot be changed. Those that may be entirely appropriate when you are thirty may be considerably less so when you are fifty and less so yet when you are sixty-five. If you are still young, you may want to seek capital appreciation above all else. As you grow older, you may consider liberal income or safety of principal much more important.

In short, at some point in your life, bonds may make a great deal of sense to you. And at almost any time, they are worth consideration. For one thing, they can often serve as excellent collateral on loans and, for this purpose, are far more acceptable than stocks. For another thing, they can provide an important means of diversifying your investment portfolio.

No investor can expect all his investments to do equally well. In fact, the typical investor can expect that he will make money from some of them, yet lose money on others. So, if he is wise, he doesn't put all his eggs in one basket. He tries to spread his risk. He diversifies his holdings.

Some investors do this by investing in a variety of stocks. But the best investors, and particularly the most affluent, usually own a combination of stocks and bonds. The nature of the combination may vary greatly in accordance with general economic conditions and the needs of the individual. But as Robert M. Baylis, vice president and director of research for The First Boston Corporation, recently put it: "We suggest to many people with balanced portfolios that they keep 25 percent of their holdings in fixed-income securities (bonds and preferred stocks) under any and all circumstances."

So far it may seem as if there were no dangers or drawbacks to investing in bonds, aside from the fact that they are not ordinarily considered the best means of increasing one's capital. Yet, like every other kind of investment, bonds do suffer from potential drawbacks.

For one thing, they can enter default. Between 1900 and 1943, the average annual default rate for corporate bonds was 1.7 percent of their face value. Between 1944 and 1965, this average annual rate slumped to 0.1 percent.* So the risk of losing principal, interest or both seems relatively small. And even this risk can be greatly reduced by investing only in bonds rated A or better.

Still and all, defaults on both corporate and municipal do occur. For example, a few years ago the Chesapeake Bridge and Tunnel Authority issued three series of bonds, of different degrees of seniority, to help pay for the 17.6-mile combination bridge and tunnel that connects the Cape Charles area with Norfolk, Virginia. The Authority's Series

---

*See *Trends in Corporate Bond Quality,* Thomas R. Atkinson, National Bureau of Economic Research, New York, 1967.

A and Series B bonds have steadily paid interest. Yet its Series C bonds have been in default for several years and, as of early 1974, were behind in their interest payments by almost $16 million.

Furthermore, even when bonds avoid default, they are not entirely free of risk. Thus it may be your intention to buy them and hold them until they mature. But your circumstances could change, forcing you to sell. In such a case, there is a risk that your holdings may be selling for less than their face value.

For example, bonds issued by the U.S. Treasury are considered the safest of all bonds. Yet even they are not free from severe price declines. Thus, between January 1967 and May 1970 the price of U.S. Treasury bonds that pay 4.25 percent in interest and that will mature in 1992 ranged from about 97 to 68. This is a decline of about 30 percent.

Interestingly, these bonds have still not made anything resembling a full recovery. In the summer of 1974, they were selling for about 72.

Take another example. In 1973 alone, bonds issued by Telex Corporation, paying 9 percent interest and due to mature in 1996, plunged from 89 to 39, a drop of fifty points.

Price drops of this magnitude are truly exceptional in the case of straight, as opposed to convertible, bonds. Yet they do occur from time to time, putting the investor who must sell such bonds at a tremendous disadvantage.

Another drawback to bonds is that they make a better buy at some times than at others. They may have been as good a buy as they have ever been in 1970, when even those rated AAA commanded interest of more than 9.25 percent. Since then, the interest rates on AAA-rated and all other bonds have fallen somewhat, then climbed back up again. Although their recent rate was very high by historical standards, there is no guarantee how long it will prevail. It could fall (or rise even higher) at any time.

This does not mean that bonds may not continue to return a good income in comparison with other fixed-income securities. But it does mean that they may not be as attractive as they have recently been.

Remember, too, that the investor has to pay federal income taxes on the interest from all bonds except muncipal (tax-exempt) bonds. This cuts into his yield.

Of course, he also has to pay federal income taxes on dividends from stocks. But when you remember that most people invest in bonds in order to obtain income and in stocks in order to obtain capital gains, you will realize that the tax on interest is more significant than the tax on dividends, although not perhaps than the tax on capital gains.

A substantial danger to investing in bonds, as to investing in almost anything else, involves speculation. Naturally, speculation also offers the greatest opportunity for profit-making. Whether the potential gains outweigh the potential drawbacks is for you to decide. In any case, there are several ways you can approach the job.

One involves trying to predict changes in the going interest rate and investing accordingly. For example, if you think that money will become more plentiful and that the interest rate will fall, you might buy certain long-term bonds. If the interest rate does fall, the price of the bonds will have to rise to bring their yields into line with those of new bonds. You can then sell the bonds and reap a capital gain.

Predicting a change in the interest rate is perhaps not as hard as predicting a change in the movement of stock prices. This is partly because bond prices and yields are directly affected by the current supply of money, partly because there is a great deal of information available about the status of the economy, likely movements in the prime interest rate and other important economic indicators. Still and all, making such a prediction is a tricky business. If the interest rate were to move upward instead of downward in an instance like the one just cited, you could lose heavily.

You can also engage in a technique known as sector swapping. Thus you may believe that certain kinds of bonds —industrial bonds, utility bonds, United States government bonds or whatever—are undervalued in relation to other kinds. So you may sell bonds that you believe are overvalued and buy those that you think are undervalued. If the undervalued bonds rise in price, you can sell them and obtain a capital gain.

To engage in this kind of trading, however, you need detailed knowledge of the usual relations in price among various groups of bonds. For example, bonds issued by the United States government or one of its agencies ordinarily yield slightly less than the best corporate bonds. This is because the guarantee of the government or one of its agencies is considered better than that of any corporation.

Even so, issues of the government and its agencies occasionally dip to a level very close or even equal to that of top-flight corporate bonds. When this happens, it may be time to buy the government or agency issues with the idea of selling them later on.

There are probably more opportunities to engage in sector swapping than in interest-rate anticipation. On the other hand, the capital gains from sector swapping are likely to be smaller.

You can also engage in what is known as pure swapping. That is, you can swap bonds in the same category—for example, one corporate bond for another that is very much like it.

The bond market is composed of thousands of issues and, as interest rates fluctuate, not all bonds respond in exactly the same way at exactly the same moment. For a short period, there may be tiny differences in their prices and yields that ordinarily wouldn't exist. So you may buy bonds that seem behind in price or yield, on the theory that they will eventually catch up with the rest of the market. You will usually be right.

For this reason, pure swapping is not a particularly risky technique. On the other hand, the gain on any single transaction is likely to be very small. Also, pure swapping requires a very detailed, up-to-the-minute knowledge of interest-rate movements and the reactions of individual bonds to these movements.

You can also buy bonds with relatively low ratings—say, bonds rated BB or B. If you do so, you will obtain a much higher rate of interest than you would if you bought bonds of higher rating. But you will be assuming that the bonds are much safer than the investment advisory organizations think they are and that the records of the issuing companies will eventually reflect this fact. If you are right, the bonds will probably rise in price sooner or later. You can then sell them for a capital gain.

All of these techniques have been employed by professional bond traders and will be again. But they are not to be recommended to most amateur investors. They require too much time and knowledge, and most of them involve a considerable amount of risk.

If you truly want to speculate, if you are really seeking big capital gains, and if you can run the risk of losing all that you invest, you will probably do better to speculate in common stocks or commodities. The returns are apt to be greater.

Professional traders may protest that just as good gains can be made by trading bonds. And they may often be right. But the opportunities to speculate in stocks or commodities are more frequent. And for reasons we will learn later on, it is usually much easier to sell 50 or 100 shares of stock or a commodity contract than it is to sell $5,000 or $10,000 worth of bonds.

There is yet another technique for speculating in bonds in the hope of making a capital gain. It is by no means risk-free. But it is probably the best method for the amateur investor to follow.

This method involves leveraging. Leveraging, of course, simply means investing with borrowed money. It is less expensive to leverage with bonds than it is with stocks because you have to put up so much less money. Thus you can often borrow from 80 to 95 percent of the value of the bonds you wish to invest in. If you invest in stocks, on the other hand, you can currently borrow no more than 50 percent.

Here is a simplified, hypothetical example of how leveraging works: An investor wants to buy five bonds put out by American Telephone & Telegraph. They pay 3.25 percent interest and are due to mature in 1984. They sell for about 68. This means their market value amounts to $3,400.

The investor puts up $780 of his own money—or 20 percent of the cost—and borrows the other $2,620 he needs. He pays annual interest of 10 percent on the loan. This amounts to $262.

Against this, he will earn annual interest of $162.50 (3.25 percent times the bonds' face value of $5,000). So his net annual outlay is reduced to about $100, plus a very small sales commission, plus taxes on the interest from the bonds. These taxes will be partly negated by the fact that he can deduct the interest on his loan on his income tax return.

Soon after he buys his bonds, the bond market rallies. Prices gradually rise about 10 points. So his bonds are now worth $3,900 instead of $3,400, and he sells them. He has made a small but neat profit of $500—less commissions, taxes and the annual net cost of his loan divided by the period of time he held it—on a total outlay less than twice that figure. This, of course, is a commendable rate of return on any investment.

Now let's look at a similar example on a much larger scale. It was suggested a few years ago by Charles J. Miller, senior partner of D.H. Blair & Company, in Robert Metz's column, Market Place, in *The New York Times*. It is reported here in paraphrased form.

An investor purchases $1 million worth of U.S. Treasury bonds known in the trade as the Gay 90's. They pay 3.5 percent interest, are due to mature in 1990 and sell for 64¼ ($642,500).

The investor puts up only $50,000 of his own money, which is perhaps $30,000 less than some brokerage houses would require. He borrows the other $592,500 he needs through a margin account with his brokerage house at annual interest of 9.5 percent. The bonds have a current yield of 5.4 percent, however, meaning that the actual cost of the loan is somewhat more than $24,000 on an annual basis ($592,500 times 4.1 percent).

So he now owns 1,000 bonds with a face value worth $1 million. His total outlay is $50,000, plus the net cost of his interest on his loan and commissions.

Within a month, the bonds climb in value a mere 5¼ points, to 69½. He sells them. Thus he makes $52,500, minus commissions and about $2,000 in interest (one-twelfth of $24,000-plus). In short, he nets about $50,000 on an investment of about $50,000, all in a month's time.

Sound like something you should emulate? Maybe so. Just remember that if the bond had slumped in price by 5-plus points instead of rising by that amount, the investor would have lost his entire investment. Such a result is probably more common than doubling one's outlay.

Bonds offer yet two other important ways of achieving

capital gains. One way involves investing in so-called discount bonds, the other in convertible bonds. The first way is clearly safer than any of the speculative ventures discussed earlier in this chapter. And both ways offer other decided advantages. They will be discussed in upcoming chapters.

So far I have largely discussed bonds in and of themselves and as they relate to certain standards, such as safety of principal. I have not discussed them as they compare to other investments. Yet probably a few words should be said about the ordinary alternatives to bonds—common and preferred stocks.

As we have already seen, over the long run of time common stocks offer a greater opportunity for capital gains than bonds do. At the same time, common stocks are ordinarily a far riskier investment.

But there is another facet to stocks that you should not overlook. They can and sometimes do return good income. Their yield is figured in the same way that the yield on bonds is, by dividing the price of the stock into its dividend. Thus, if a stock sells for $50 a share and pays an annual dividend of $3, it yields 6 percent ($50 into $3).

Unfortunately, the yields on common stocks rarely equal the yields on bonds. What's more, the yield on a common stock is much less certain than the yield on a bond. The dividend on the stock may be slashed or eliminated altogether. The interest due on the bond cannot be changed. Nonetheless, a number of companies in this country have paid dividends without interruption for many decades, and some have never cut these dividends.

Preferred stocks are a better bet than common stocks. Historically, in fact, they have been the chief alternative investment to bonds.

Like bonds, they are considered senior securities. In other words, if the company involved ever goes bankrupt, its preferred stockholders will be paid off before its common stockholders, although not, of course, before its bondholders.

Like bonds, they also pay a fixed rate of return, which is called a dividend. And they usually carry a guarantee that their owners will receive this dividend even if the company's common stockholders receive nothing.

Like bonds, they also tend to move in narrow price ranges. For example, during the first six months of 1973, the price of the common stock of Atlantic Richfield ranged from 66 to 91, while the price of its preferred stock ranged only from 50 to 55.

Finally, like bonds, preferred stocks are rated by investment advisory organizations. The ratings on the two kinds of investments carry the same meaning.

So preferred stocks tend to meet the same two criteria that most bonds do. They provide considerable safety of principal, plus a liberal income. But they also offer very little chance of capital appreciation.

Thus it is safe to say that if you are considering investing in corporate bonds, you should also look into the preferred stocks, if any, of the issuing companies. By definition, you can assume that the bonds are a little safer than the preferred stocks. And this is not only because bondholders have first claim on the company's assets in event of bankruptcy, but also because the company may omit dividend payments to its preferred stockholders in a given year or even a series of years. If the stocks are cumulative preferred, however, the company will be required to make up the dividends in later years if it possibly can.

You will probably also find that the bonds yield more than the preferred stocks do. How much more will depend on the company and on conditions in the bond market. The figure may range from a few to many basis points.

A basis point equals one-hundredth of 1 percent. In

Cht 4 -

other words, 100 basis points equal 1 percent.

Whether you should buy the bonds or the stocks depends on your individual investment requirements, plus how the bonds and stocks stack up against each other in terms of safety and yield. All other things being equal, some investment experts think you should choose the preferred stocks only if they are yielding 1 percent more than the bonds. On the other hand, it's well to remember that it's very easy to buy or sell, say, $2,000 worth of preferred stock, while it can be difficult or costly to buy or sell less than $5,000 worth of bonds.

What, then, are the main things we have learned from this chapter. First, no one should invest in bonds or anything else unless he has sufficient money to live on, plus funds set aside for a rainy day. Second, bonds should interest most investors but at certain times in their lives more than at others. Third, the great, lasting attractions of bonds involve safety of principal and liberal income. Fourth, it is possible to speculate in bonds with an eye to achieving capital gains, but this usually requires considerable knowledge of the bond market. Finally, there are other investments that may serve your purposes better than bonds at any given point in time.

End of Chpt. 4

Chapter 5

Corporate Bonds: A Growing Boom

At the end of 1947, the volume of corporate bonds in this country's secondary market amounted to $14.1 billion. This figure includes only publicly offered, as opposed to privately placed, bonds. It includes only straight, as opposed to convertible, bonds. And it reflects the bonds' face rather than their market values.

By late 1972, some twenty-five years later, this figure had soared to $140.4 billion. In other words, within less than three decades, the size of the corporate bond market swelled tenfold.

Furthermore, there is no end in sight. Salomon Brothers estimates that some $172.2 billion of corporate bonds will be outstanding by the end of 1974. And this figure is expected to rise even further throughout this decade.

Why this huge increase in corporate debt? Largely because of rising costs and falling profits, many corporations are generating less cash than they once did. At the same time, their need for funds to finance the construction of new plants and factories, to buy new equipment and to obtain more working capital is increasing all the time.

The rate of increase in publicly offered corporate bonds now far exceeds the rate of increase in privately placed corporate bonds. In the early 1950s, the volumes outstanding of the two groups of bonds were about equal. But a gap soon began to appear, and it has slowly become wider and wider. As a result, the market in publicly offered bonds is now more than twice as large as the market in privately placed bonds.

As you can guess, the public market at any one time offers thousands of issues to choose among. These issues vary greatly in terms of interest rates, maturity dates and other factors. They also vary in terms of the industries that issue them.

Nonetheless, the Salomon Brothers 1972 study shows that the market is dominated by utility issues. In 1972 these issues accounted for 59 percent of the total volume of corporate bonds. Next came industrial bonds with 26 percent, then finance bonds with 11 percent and finally transportation bonds with 4 percent.

The reason the utilities dominate the market is quite simple. Their demand for capital to finance new construction and new equipment is tremendous and never-ending regardless of how profitable they may be in any given period.

From the investor's standpoint, this dominance is a good thing. Although most bonds receive high ratings from the investment advisory organizations, utility bonds tend to receive the highest of all.

Thus, in 1972 some 83 percent of all corporate issues were rated A or better by Standard & Poor's. Yet some 90 percent of all utility issues carried one of the A ratings. And another 8 percent were rated BBB.

All this may now be changing somewhat because the earnings of many of the nation's utilities have recently been under pressure. In April 1974 Standard & Poor's reduced the rating on Cleveland Electric Illuminating's bonds from AAA to AA. As a result the number of utilities rated triple-A by both Moody's and Standard & Poor's was reduced to six. As recently as 1970, no fewer than sixteen utilities carried triple-A ratings.

Obviously, however, there are many other very good corporate bonds around. How should you go about picking among them? We have already discussed or touched upon three of the four most important factors you should consider.

One, of course, is safety of principal. Naturally, you can go a long way toward determining a bond's safety of principal by ascertaining its credit rating. As you know, a bond with a rating of AAA, AA or A is considered very safe.

Another factor is yield. In all probability, you will want the highest possible yield. Presumably you will also want maximum safety of principal. Yet the higher a bond's rating, the lower its yield is apt to be. So you will have to compromise.

Even so, the compromise will not have to be that drastic. You can find many bonds with very considerable safety of principal and very good yields, even though they may not provide the greatest possible degree of each.

The third factor to consider is maturity. Thus you may be willing to invest your money for a long period of time —say, the twenty or thirty years for which many bonds are issued. Or you may want to invest for a much shorter period—say, ten years.

If you want to buy a brand-new bond, its maturity date will have a definite effect on its interest rate and yield. The further the maturity date is in the future, the more interest the bond will be apt to pay, at least when normal market conditions prevail. That is simply because the issuer will have use of the money it borrows for a longer period of time.

To cite an example, the Southern Pacific Transportation Company recently issued $15 million worth of equipment-trust certificates, some of which will mature each and every year between 1975 and 1989. Those due to mature in 1975 were originally priced to yield 7.5 percent, those in 1980 to yield 7.6 percent, those in 1985 to yield 7.8 percent and those in 1989 to yield 8 percent.

Of course, you don't have to buy new bonds. You can buy those that have been traded for some period of time and that are due to mature in seven years or eleven years or at the end of some other period in the future. The interest rates on these bonds will also have been set partly in terms of their maturity dates. But the fact that you may buy them several years after they were issued will have no effect on the interest you receive, although it may, of course, affect the yield.

The final factor you will want to consider is a bond's call provisions. There was a day when only a minority of corporate bonds had such provisions. But all that has changed since World War II. Today most new bonds are callable after a specified period of time.

Naturally, the issuing companies don't always exercise this option. But when they don't, it is usually because they will not be able to issue new bonds at a lower rate of interest. They will have to pay the same rate or one that is even higher.

This brings up the one great disadvantage that utility bonds suffer in relation to other corporate bonds. Most, although not all, utility bonds can be called in after five years. Most, although not all, other corporate bonds can be called in only after ten years.

Whatever the exact terms of a bond's call provisions, they usually place a ceiling on the price to which a bond may rise in the open market. In other words, investors are usually unwilling to pay more for a bond than its call price.

Nonetheless, call provisions are probably here to stay. So if you want to invest your money for ten years, you will want to be cautious about purchasing a bond that can be called in in five. Or if you want to invest your money for five years, you will want to be cautious about purchasing a bond that has already been trading for two years and that can be refunded in another three.

All these factors—safety, yield, maturity and call provisions—should probably be weighed separately rather than together. In so doing, you will rapidly reduce the bond universe. Even so, you will find a wealth of bonds to choose from.

Thus, if you confine yourself to bonds rated AAA, you will still be able to find many in that category with different yields, maturities and call provisions. Or, if you confine yourself to bonds yielding, say, 9 percent or more, you will still be able to find many with different ratings, maturities and call provisions.

In 1969 a new and different kind of bond came on the market. It had been virtually unheard of before, but in its first year alone it captured nearly 7 percent of all public corporate bond financing.

The new kind of bond differed from other bonds in two important respects: it was noncallable. And it had a very short maturity. Some of the new bonds were issued for three, four or six years. But most were issued for five. So they were quickly dubbed five-year bonds.

There were several reasons why such bonds began to be issued. First, a company could pay somewhat less interest than it would have had to pay on bonds with longer terms and also somewhat less interest than it would probably have had to pay a bank. Second, in issuing such bonds, a company could bet that interest rates would dip within the ensuing five years and that it could then pay off the bonds and issue new ones at longer terms and lower rates. Third, issuers of these bonds did not have to make them subject to call and thus to possible payment of call premiums.

Despite their instant popularity, five-year bonds were denounced by a number of investment bankers. Some called the bonds a gimmick. Others pointed out that their issuers were merely delaying the inevitability of seeking long-term financing.

Whatever the cause, five-year bonds faded considerably in popularity but have since made something of a comeback. Interest in this kind of financing conceivably could increase even further in the future.

But remember this: you may be better off to buy a long-term bond that can be refunded in five years than to buy a short-term bond that will mature in five years. That's because the former may return more interest than the latter if they were both issued at the same time. In addition, the longer-term bond will return you a premium should it be called in.

There is another kind of corporate bond that may, and probably should, interest you much more than a five-year bond. It's known as a discount bond. And as its very name implies, it is a bond that sells at a discount from its face value. As you know, this value is usually $1,000 (100).

Do not assume, however, that all bonds that sell at discounts are discount bonds as that term is commonly used. At various times, many bonds sell at discounts merely because bond prices in general are depressed. Others sell at discounts because some question has arisen as to whether the issuing corporations will really be able to pay them off when they mature.

A true discount bond is a special breed of cat. Often it is an older bond that pays a very low rate of interest, perhaps only 3 percent or even less. Often, too, it is due to mature within only three or four years.

Many such bonds were issued during World War II or in the years immediately thereafter. At the time, the U.S. Treasury held interest rates artificially low in order to reduce the interest that had to be paid on the federal debt.

But in later years interest rates rose substantially. As a result, the older bonds had to drop in price. Otherwise, their yields wouldn't have matched the yields on the newer bonds, and they wouldn't have aroused much interest among investors.

This brings up the first and greatest advantage of discount bonds. They provide an opportunity for capital gain. Furthermore, barring default, the opportunity for capital gain is a sure-fire thing, involving no speculation whatsoever.

Discount bonds provide this opportunity because the corporations that issued them will eventually have to pay them off at their face value. Thus, if you invest in discount bonds before they mature, you will reap the difference between the discounted price you pay for them and their face value.

Furthermore, this capital gain will be taxed at the capital gains rate. As you know, this rate is much lower than that levied on interest and other ordinary income.

You should understand, however, that not all discount bonds are due to mature in only a few years. Some may not mature for fifteen years or even more. But they differ from other bonds that may be selling at a discount in that they were issued when interest rates were considerably lower.

For example, Philadelphia Electric has some discount bonds outstanding that will mature in 1994. They pay interest of 4.5 percent and, as this is written, were selling for 50.

You may wonder how much chance there is that such a bond will be called in. The chance is slight. A corporation is not likely to call in a bond that is selling at a sizable discount because it would have to pay it off at its face value. It would thus lose the money it had borrowed. And if it had to borrow more, it would undoubtedly have to pay substantially greater interest.

You should also understand that the closer a discount bond approaches its maturity date, the more apt it is to rise in price. Everybody knows that when it matures it will be worth its face value.

To look at the whole matter another way, if you want to seek capital gains, you will be better off to buy discount bonds that won't mature for a number of years into the future than to buy those that will mature in only one or two years. The further off a discount bond's maturity date is, the deeper its discount is apt to be.

A case in point: Continental Natural Gas bonds, paying 3.25 percent interest and due to mature in 1976, were selling in the summer of 1974 for 90. But American Telephone & Telegraph bonds, paying exactly the same interest and due to mature in 1984, were selling for 62.

Observes Frank P. Wendt, president of John Nuveen & Co.: "Never overlook discount bonds. They have an extraordinary potential for capital gain when long-term interest rates decline and prices rise. They provide the additional advantage of protection against refunding. Therefore, the potential for gain is not held down by an early refunding date or a relatively low call price."

Are there then no drawbacks to discount bonds? Certainly there are.

For one thing, you may not buy them near the bottom of the market. After your purchase, interest rates may rise, pushing bond prices down further. If you had delayed your purchase, you might have been able to buy the bonds at an even lower price and thus increased the amount of your potential capital gain. Thus timing is important to the purchase of discount bonds, just as it is to almost every other kind of investment.

What's more, you should not consider discount bonds if your primary investment goal is liberal income. By definition, discount bonds pay less interest than other kinds of bonds.

Finally, you should be aware that, for all practical purposes, there is a limit on the amount of capital gain you can achieve by investing in discount bonds. That limit is equal to their face value, for a bond of this stripe is not apt to rise much, if at all, above that value.

So, if you are primarily interested in capital gains, you may do better to invest in common stocks. The potential will be greater, possibly much greater, although it's only fair to add that you could end up suffering a loss instead of achieving a gain.

Thus the real strength of discount bonds is that the capital gains they offer are virtually assured. Common stocks offer nothing so certain.

What are the most important things we have learned from this chapter? First, the corporate bond market has been growing at a very rapid rate and is almost certain to continue to do so throughout this decade. Second, corporate bonds are available for investment in a wide range of ratings, yields, interest rates and maturity dates. Third, corporate bonds selling at discounts from their face values offer the possibility of almost sure-fire capital gains.

End of Chpt. 5

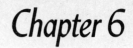
Chapter 6

Convertible Bonds:
The Ideal Investment?

There is an old saying that convertible bonds make the ideal investment. Like all old sayings, it contains an element of truth. And like all old sayings, it is subject to many qualifications.

The reason convertible bonds are often called the ideal investment lies in their very nature. They are bonds that can be converted into a specific number of shares of stock —usually common, although sometimes preferred. Thus they are part bond and part stock.

In theory, at least, they are believed to partake of the best of both possible worlds. In bull markets they are supposed to act like stocks and enjoy rises in price. In bear markets they are supposed to act like bonds and resist declines in price.

Often enough this theory works out. For example, between May 1970 and April 1971, Baxter Laboratories' common stock rose in price 35 percent, while its convertible bonds went up more than 33 percent. During the same period J.C. Penney's common stock rose nearly 61 percent, while its convertible bonds went up more than 50 percent.

Similarly, during part of 1969, American Machine & Foundry's common stock fell nearly 26 percent. But its convertible bonds went down only 5 percent. During the same period Air Reduction's common stock slumped 41 percent. But its convertible bonds dropped only 24 percent.

Nonetheless, the theory often proves erroneous, to at least some degree. Convertibles sometimes go up nowhere nearly as far or as fast as their related common stocks. And on occasion they fall in price even more precipitously.

Even at their best they are subject to much wider price fluctuations than regular bonds are. For example, in 1973 Chase Manhattan Realty convertibles of 1990 ranged from 256 to 170, finishing the year at the low. And Cooper Laboratories' convertibles of 1992 varied from 102 to 35, ending at 40.

Still wider fluctuations could be cited. The point is, price swings of this magnitude are not considered unusual among convertible bonds. But they are considered unusual among regular bonds.

Before proceeding further, let's learn more exactly what convertibles are and why they act as they do. Unfortunately, they are one of the hardest of all investments to understand. Fortunately, we already know a great deal about them. That's because they have many of the same features as regular bonds.

For example, they have a face value. This face value is usually equal to $1,000. Yet it is commonly listed as 100.

Convertible bonds also pay a fixed rate of interest. Because they are convertible, however, this rate is almost invariably less than what it would be on a regular bond issued by the same company at the same time. The difference may range from less than one to several percentage points.

The bonds also have maturity dates, at which time they will be redeemed at their face values, no matter at what prices they have traded in the meantime. Although the terms of convertibles may vary widely, they generally run to twenty or twenty-five years.

In addition, the bonds usually carry call prices. As you can guess, these prices are somewhat in excess of the bonds' face values.

Finally, convertibles have a so-called *investment value.* This is a term we have not run across before. It refers to the price a convertible bond would probably sell at if it were merely a bond and not a bond that was convertible into stock—that is, the price it would sell at on the basis of yield alone.

Unlike face values, interest rates, maturity dates and call prices, investment values are not immutably fixed nor are they made part of convertible bonds' indenture provisions. Rather they represent the best estimates of investment advisory organizations like Moody's and Standard & Poor's. These estimates are based on credit ratings, interest rates and other factors. Because these ratings and rates sometimes change, investment values sometimes do so, too, moving either upward or downward.

Why is a convertible's investment value important?

For one thing, the difference, if any, between a bond's market price and its investment value is one important factor to consider in deciding whether it would make a sound investment. The larger the difference, the less protection the bond will provide against a fall in price.

For another thing, a bond's investment value is supposed to provide a floor beneath its price. After all, this value is set largely in terms of what other bonds of comparable stature sell for.

Yet to say that the floor usually holds up is not to say that it always does so. If the issuing company defaults on interest payments or if the Federal Reserve System takes action that increases interest rates, a bond's price may dip below its investment value, in which case the value may change.

As we have noted, a convertible bond carries a special right: the right to convert it into a specified number of shares of the issuing company's preferred or common stock. Thus the bond may be convertible into five or fourteen or twenty-three or some other number of shares of stock. Whatever the exact number, they constitute the bond's *conversion ratio.*

Typically, this right extends throughout the life of the bond and remains constant throughout that life. But there are exceptions to this rule and, if you ever consider investing in such bonds, you should familiarize yourself with their conversion terms.

Occasionally, a bond can't be converted until several months or years after it has been issued. More often, it is convertible into steadily smaller amounts of stock. For example, it may be convertible into fifteen shares of stock over the first ten years of its life, ten shares over the next five, and five shares over the last five. Sometimes the conversion privilege expires altogether before the bond matures.

The value of the number of shares for which a convertible can be exchanged give it a *conversion value,* which is not to be confused with its conversion ratio. The conversion value is equal to the price of the company's stock multiplied by the number of shares for which the bond may be exchanged. For example, if the stock is selling at 50 and each bond is convertible into five shares, the bond's conversion value is 250 (five shares times $50 a share).

A bond's conversion value is important for several reasons. First, it increases when the price of the common stock increases, thus pulling the price of the bond upward in a bull market. Simple arithmetic shows why. If the price of the stock mentioned above were to increase from 50 to 75, the conversion value of the bond would have to go up proportionately, to 375 (five shares times $75). Second, a bond will rarely sell for less than its conversion value. In fact, it will usually sell for more. Thus the difference, if any, between a bond's market price and its conversion value will be another important factor in deciding whether it would make a sound investment. The larger the difference, the less potential the bond will have for increasing in price.

This difference, if any, is known as the *conversion premium* and is often expressed as a percentage. As this is written, Western Air Lines' convertible bonds of 1993 have a conversion premium of 11 percent, representing the difference between the market price of the bonds and the value of the shares of stock into which they may be converted.

Thus we have three conversion terms: conversion ratio, referring to the number of shares into which a bond may be converted; conversion value, referring to the value of the shares into which it may be converted; and conversion premium, referring to the difference between the bond's market price and its conversion value.

Now why do companies issue convertible bonds?

Sometimes they issue convertibles because they aren't able to bring out a bond issue in any other fashion. Perhaps they already have a lot of straight bonds outstanding. Another might make a glut on the market. Or perhaps the market is temporarily unreceptive to new bond issues. Or perhaps investors have reservations about the soundness of the issuers. In the latter two cases, the conversion privilege provides a sweetener. It makes the bonds more attractive than they otherwise would be.

Sometimes companies issue convertibles because they can pay lower rates of interest than they would have to pay on straight bonds. Over the years, the difference in rates may save millions of dollars.

Sometimes companies issue convertibles because they hope buyers will eventually convert them into stock. In such case, the companies will no longer have any debt to pay off. Bondholders will have become stockholders. It is no problem to make the exchange. Brokers handle the job routinely.

Indeed, corporations have been known to force their bondholders to convert. As we will see more fully in a moment, a company is in a position to do this when its convertible is selling for considerably more than its call price. Bondholders who don't convert or sell their holdings may lose a great deal of money.

Finally, and most important, companies sometimes issue convertibles because they don't want to issue common stock. Perhaps they don't want to dilute the value of the common stock they already have outstanding by issuing more shares. Or perhaps they don't want to pay the dividends they would probably have to pay if they issued stock. The interest on bonds can be deducted before corporate taxes are computed. The dividends on stock must be paid out of post-tax income. The difference can be substantial.

For all these reasons, the convertible bond market is popular. Certainly it is a market that should interest you.

You might be interested in it because you want more protection than you would obtain if you invested in common stock. Convertibles are senior securities. In case of default, other bondholders will probably have prior claim on the company's assets. But convertible bondholders will have a claim senior to that of stockholders. Furthermore, if there is no default, you will have a guarantee that you will at least get back the face value of the bonds—more, if they are called in before maturity.

You might also be interested in convertibles because you want additional income. The income will not be as great as what you could obtain from a straight bond. But the yield is almost certain to be more than that on the related common stock.

Finally, while enjoying both of the above benefits, you may hope to achieve capital gains. Such gains can be every bit as sizable as those you might achieve by investing in common stock. Indeed, the conversion privilege is the outstanding feature of convertible bonds—the feature that makes them different from and, in some ways, more attractive than regular bonds.

Thus we see more fully why convertible bonds are sometimes termed the ideal investment and said to partake of the best of both possible worlds. They often prove especially attractive when the stock market's course seems uncertain—when the investor thinks it may go up, but wants protection against the possibility that it will go down.

Are there then no dangers to convertible bonds? There are plenty.

Different investment counselors may give different advice on the purchase of convertibles, depending on their viewpoints, the outlook for the stock market and an investor's individual needs. But on two points, you will find almost universal agreement.

First, be cautious about buying convertibles if safety of principal and liberal income are very important to you. By definition, regular bonds are usually safer and provide more income. In this connection, a key factor to consider is whether the convertible is selling above its investment value and, if so, by how much. The larger the premium is, the less protection you will have against a downward movement in prices.

Second, never buy convertibles unless you have good reason to believe in the soundness of the related stock. A convertible cannot be considered in a vacuum. It must be considered together with the stock. Their fates are inevitably intertwined. If the stock rises in price, so will the bond. If the stock falls in price, the bond will follow suit.

Another danger lies in the fact that convertibles of questionable merit often flood the market. This is especially apt to occur during bull markets, when many second- and third-line companies try to take advantage of investor euphoria by rushing convertibles out.

Then too, even the best convertible bonds are subject to the same market forces as regular bonds are. Thus, if interest rates rise, bond prices will usually fall.

Finally, there is sometimes a danger that a convertible will not be protected against dilution. In other words, the issuing company may split its stock, pay a stock dividend or merge with another company. Against such eventualities, a convertible's indenture will ordinarily require that an appropriate adjustment be made in the conversion ratio. But there have been exceptions to this rule. And these exceptions should be watched for.

There are yet other dangers to convertibles. They will become more apparent as we consider what makes a good convertible. When should you consider buying such? And when should you consider converting?

As we have seen, a good convertible has a very sound company behind it. Among other things, this means that the company earns more than the interest it must pay on all its senior securities, several times over.

A good convertible also has a sound future ahead of it. In particular, this means that the outlook for its related common stock is bright.

A good convertible offers some protection against a fall in price. In this connection, a convertible that is selling only, say, 15 percent above its investment value offers considerable protection against a fall in price. A convertible that is selling for 40 percent or more above its investment value offers only modest protection.

A good convertible also offers a good chance for appreciation in price. The extent of this opportunity will be related, in considerable measure, to the size of the conversion premium. In this connection, a premium of 50 percent or more is normally considered large.

That means the common stock may be a better buy. In buying the convertible, you may be paying more for the conversion privilege than it's worth, although it's important to add that some good convertibles carry conversion premiums well in excess of 50 percent.

The point is, when a convertible sells for more than its conversion value, it's apt to increase in price less rapidly than the corresponding stock. The bond cannot keep going indefinitely upward. If and when the stock starts to rise in price, the bond will already be selling for relatively more. So its premium over conversion value will tend to narrow rather than to widen.

Finally, and perhaps most important of all, if a bond is selling well above its call price, it may be called in. Then you may lose considerable money.

Take an example. Some years ago, a typewriter manufacturer's convertibles were selling for 125. At that time, their conversion value was about 117. Although this premium over conversion value was not overly worrisome, the bonds had a call price of 106. And when they were suddenly called in, their open-market price quickly tumbled from 125 to 117, which represented their real worth.

The investor then had three choices: he could turn them in at the call price, he could sell them at the new open-market price, or he could convert them into stock. Either of the latter two steps was preferable to the first. Even so, if he had purchased ten such bonds at their old market price of 125, he lost about $800 on the sale or conversion.

Now let's put all the terms we have been studying together and view them in light of a particular bond that Standard & Poor's recommended early in 1974. The convertible in question was issued by Sherwin-Williams, the big paint manufacturer. It pays interest of 6.25 percent and is due to mature in 1995.

It carries a rating of BBB, and Standard & Poor's said it then had an investment value of 77. As we have seen, this means that the bond is not likely to tumble below that level in a bear market assuming that the credit standing of the issuer and interest rates remain constant. In addition, the bond had a conversion value of 78¼, meaning that this was the value of the stock into which it could be converted. Finally, it had a call price of 105.

In the market, the bond was selling for 94. So what were the potential risks and rewards?

Well, the bond was selling for only 17 points more than its investment value. So, although there was risk in making a purchase, it did not seem unduly large.

Yet the bond was also selling for some 20 percent more than its conversion value. You can find convertibles with conversion premiums exceeding 100 percent. So this particular premium was not a whopping one. Yet it was big enough for Standard & Poor's to term it "sizable."

Nonetheless, the investment advisory organization said the related common stock, which was selling for 26, was soundly priced. Indeed, it thought the stock might rise because of the company's long-term prospects. So it termed the bond retainable for "potential long-term appreciation."

In any case, a purchaser would have paid less for the bond than its face value. And there would have been little likelihood that it would be called in because companies rarely call in bonds that are not selling for a good deal more than their call prices.

We have now applied several tests to convertibles—their market prices in relation to their investment values, conversion values and call prices. It should be obvious that few bonds meet all these tests perfectly. Some compromise is often in order. How much of a compromise should be made depends on your needs and wishes, plus conditions in the market.

Suggests Ronald D. Bechky, an assistant vice president in the convertible bond trading department of Merrill Lynch, Pierce, Fenner & Smith: "Investors in convertibles who are interested in capital gains should seek bonds with low conversion premiums, regardless of the size of the bonds' investment value premiums. More conservative investors should seek bonds with low investment value premiums, regardless of the size of the bonds' conversion premiums."

Once you buy, when, if ever, should you convert? The best answer is: rarely. In fact, only two occasions come quickly to mind. You must convert or sell—or lose money—if the issuer calls in its convertibles when they are selling above their call price. And you may want to convert if you are very interested in good yields and the issuer's stock starts to yield more than its bonds.

Otherwise, there's not much point in converting. If you are seeking capital gains, the bonds will usually be safer than the related stock. After all, you always have the bonds' face value to fall back on. And if you want to sell the bonds and take your profits, you will probably do as well to sell them directly as to convert them, then sell the stock.

The suggestions in this chapter represent basic advice on investing in convertibles. There are more sophisticated techniques available. Often they involve hedging. For example, an investor may buy a convertible and at the same time sell the related stock short—that is, borrow some from his broker, sell it, then plan to buy it back at what he expects will be a lower price.

Techniques like this are often designed to take advantage of price differentials in two or more securities issued by the same company. They not only require expert timing, but also a sophisticated knowledge of the bond market. They are not to be recommended to the typical investor.

What should you take away from this chapter? First, you should remember that by putting your money in convertibles, you give up some of the safety and some of the income you would receive from regular bonds in exchange for the prospect of above-average capital gains. Second, you should remember that convertibles often fluctuate in price to a far greater degree than regular bonds do. This may be no great cause for concern if you buy a convertible at or below its face value and plan to hold it until maturity. But it should be cause for considerable concern if you have to sell earlier. Finally, you should remember at least two of the technical terms used in connection with convertibles. One is investment value, the level below which a convertible's price will not usually fall because it represents its estimated worth as a straight bond. The other is conversion value, the convertible's worth in terms of the stock for which it may be exchanged.

End of Chpt. 6

goes from pg 86 to pg 106 = 21 pgs

Chapter 7

Municipal Bonds:
The Rich Man's Darlings

Next to bonds issued by the United States government or its agencies, municipal bonds are usually considered the safest of all senior securities. That's because they are frequently backed by the full tax power of the state or city that issues them.

Yet in recent years, the common assumption that municipal bonds are very safe has had to be qualified. There are two closely related reasons why.

There was a day when the municipal bond market was dominated by institutional investors, in particular by commercial banks. In fact, it still is dominated by these investors. Yet, when the stock market went into a decline a few years ago, many individuals began to consider other kinds of investments. Municipal bonds suddenly proved very popular. And today individuals own nearly one-third of the total value of all municipal bonds and notes outstanding.

As the number of individual investors increased, some municipal bond dealers began to prey on them. These dealers touted bonds of inferior quality, lied about the true nature of the issuers and misrepresented prices, yields, maturities and heaven knows what. One popular trick was to refer to certain municipals as "of a quality"—a verbal play upon the A ratings issued by Moody's and Standard & Poor's and a flagrant misrepresentation of the caliber of the bonds.

In 1972 the president of the Florida Securities Dealers Association estimated that at least twenty firms in his state alone were using unethical and fraudulent practices to sell municipal bonds. A year later, the Securities & Exchange Commission won an injunction against a Memphis, Tennessee, firm that forbad it from violating the antifraud provisions of the nation's securities laws. The firm had been charged with misrepresenting bonds and selling them at markups as high as 78 percent above market prices. A few months later a West Orange, New Jersey, firm that had spent hundreds of thousands of dollars on television commercials to attract individual investors was forced into involuntary bankruptcy. It, too, faced an array of charges from the SEC.

Despite all this, it would be grossly unfair to imply that the municipal bond industry has become rife with corruption. In fact, the unethical dealers have been relatively few in number. But they have received a great deal of publicity, and their emergence points up one fact you should never forget if you ever consider purchasing municipal bonds: be very sure of the reputability of the dealer from whom you make your purchase.

The basic problem is that, unlike the corporate bond market, the municipal bond market is virtually unregulated by the United States government, the Securities & Exchange Commission or any other agency. Until recent years this lack of regulation was not considered particularly dangerous because the market was so heavily dominated by institutions, and it was presumed that they could take care of themselves.

But, as more individuals entered the market, attitudes began to change. As a result, the SEC recently sought and got more regulatory powers from Congress. Even so, you have reason to be wary, especially if a municipal bond house telephones you unsolicited.

Now let's examine municipals themselves. Fortunately, they have many of the same features as corporates. And the few differences between them are much easier to understand than the differences between corporates and convertibles.

Municipals are issued not only by cities, but also by towns and villages, by states, possessions and territories, and by various public authorities on all these levels of government. The latter include bridge and tunnel, housing, port and other kinds of authorities.

These various bodies issue bonds for all kinds of purposes. Yet they usually do so to finance new construction, ranging from jetports to parking facilities, from public transportation to sports arenas, from waterworks to waste disposal plants. These bodies also seek money in the same way corporations do. They go to an underwriter and entrust him with the job of bringing their bonds to market.

The resulting issues possess almost all of the features that corporate bonds do. In other words, they carry the names of the issuers, bear fixed rates of interest payable over the life of the bonds, are issued at certain initial prices and thereafter trade at whatever prices they can command in the secondary market. They also boast current yields and yields to maturity, and they can usually be called in before they mature.

How, then, do municipals differ from corporates?

First and foremost, the interest from municipals is exempt from taxation. For this reason, the bonds are frequently referred to as tax-exempts. Indeed, the terms "municipals" and "tax-exempts" are used so interchangeably that it is hard to say which is more common.

This exemption is the chief reason why municipal bonds are considered among the most attractive of all investments. Because of it, municipals carry much lower rates of interest than corporates. Often the difference amounts to three percentage points or more among bonds of comparable quality.

When it's said that municipals are tax-exempt, it's meant that they are exempt from federal income taxes. Yet they are usually also exempt from income taxes imposed by state and local governments when purchased by individuals living in the states of issue.

For example, if you live in New York State, you probably would not have to pay state or local taxes on any bonds issued by any governmental unit or authority in that state. But you probably would have to pay taxes on bonds issued by or in another eastern or a midwestern or a far western state. Since state laws vary somewhat, it is usually wise to check the laws in one's own state before purchasing municipals.

The only bonds exempt from all state and local taxes are those issued by the District of Columbia, the Commonwealth of Puerto Rico, Guam, the Virgin Islands and any American Indian nation. These bonds are known as triple-exempts (from federal, state and local taxes). And as you can guess, they are very popular.

Why are municipal bonds made tax-exempt? One reason arises from various rulings made by the United States Supreme Court. As far back as 1819, in a case known as McCulloch v. Maryland, the court ruled that the United

States government could not tax the means or instrumentalities of the various states—and vice versa. As Chief Justice John Marshall saw it, the power to tax was the power to destroy, and his court ruled that neither the federal nor the state governments had the right to tax or destroy the other. The court has reaffirmed this ruling many times over the years.

There is an additional reason why municipal bonds are tax-exempt. If they were not, they would have to return considerably more interest in order to attract investors. This interest would have to be paid by taxpayers, thus pushing up property, sales and other local taxes. As a result, many much-needed bond issues would never be voted into existence.

Municipal bonds also differ from corporate bonds in that they are usually *serial bonds.* Most corporates, by contrast, are *term bonds.* Serial bonds mature in annual installments. Term bonds mature all at once except, of course, when they are retired periodically by means of sinking fund payments.

The State of Maryland, for example, recently issued $50 million worth of municipal bonds in serial form. Some will mature in 1977, some in 1978, some in 1979 and so on right through 1989.

When municipal bonds are brought out in this fashion, either their interest rates or their yields usually rise over the bonds' life. In other words, the bonds with later maturities usually return more than those with earlier maturities.

Why are municipals usually issued in serial form? First, it enables the cost of a civic improvement to be shared among its present and future beneficiaries. Second, it reduces the overall cost. An underwriter can do better by breaking an issue into short-term, medium-term and long-term bonds and pricing each category according to the going interest rates affecting that category.

Issuance of municipals in this fashion is also a boon to investors. They don't have to put their money into bonds that won't mature for twenty or thirty years. They can put it into bonds that will mature in one year or four years or twelve years or whatever period they like. Or they can spread their investment over several maturities so that they can get some of their principal back each and every year or every few years.

As we have already seen, most corporate bonds issued at the present time are registered bonds. Most municipals, however, are bearer or coupon bonds and are presumed to belong to whoever possesses them. This makes it doubly important that they be kept in a safety deposit box or otherwise safeguarded. Although thefts may be infrequent, they do occur.

Take what *The New York Times* tagged as The Case of the Albuquerque Eights. In 1970 Albuquerque, New Mexico, issued $9.2 million worth of bonds to finance a convention center. Some of the bonds paid interest of 8 percent.

A few weeks after they were issued, a Mrs. Ruth Gitten of New York City purchased $45,000 worth from Bache & Co., one of the nation's leading brokerage houses. Bache mailed her the bonds by registered mail.

Unfortunately, they never reached her. They were kept in a United States post office safe over a weekend, and somebody broke into the post office and carted off the entire safe. When it was recovered, the bonds were missing.

They turned up in the hands of one Benjamin S. Haggett Jr., a vice president of the Meadow Brook National Bank in nearby Queens. Haggett pledged the bonds as collateral on a loan from the Republic National Bank of New York. Later he asked Republic National to sell the bonds and pay off the note, which it did. The bonds were then sold from one securities concern to another and finally to the First National Bank in Albuquerque, which happened to be the agent that paid interest on them.

First National discovered that they were stolen when one of its departments tried to obtain interest payments from another department. The bank then traced the bonds back to Republic National and Benjamin Haggett. Nearly a year after the theft, Bache repaid Mrs. Gitten for her loss, and she deposited the money in a savings account. Seventeen months after that, Haggett was sentenced to five years in prison for possessing bonds he knew had been stolen.

As we have seen, most corporates are issued in denominations of $1,000. Most new municipals, on the other hand, are issued in denominations of $5,000. Nonetheless, their prices are still listed as if they had par values of $1,000— i.e., at 100 or something above or below that figure.

Yet, if you actually talk to a dealer about municipals, he will refer to most of them in terms of their yield to maturity or, as the trade puts it, on a yield basis. For example, a typical quote might be: Maine State Housing Authority, 5½s of 11/15/82 at a 4.50 basis. This would indicate that these bonds pay 5.5 percent interest, mature on November 15, 1982, and will yield 4.5 percent if held to maturity.

A reasonable number of corporate bonds are listed on the New York Stock Exchange, the American Stock Exchange or one of the regional stock exchanges. Almost all municipal bonds, by contrast, are traded in the over-the-counter market.

According to the Municipal Financial Officers Association, there are some 120,000 separate municipal bond issues available. Yet many are never traded or are traded only occasionally. That's because investors tend to purchase them, then hold them until maturity.

Because of the size of the market and the somewhat limited trading in seasoned issues, municipal bond prices are almost never listed in daily newspapers. You can only ascertain their prices by consulting a bond dealer or your stockbroker.

Either one is likely to refer to *The Blue List of Current Municipal Offerings,* a thick, daily publication informally known as the blue list. It lists municipal bonds that dealers are trying to sell, plus the bonds' offering prices, yields and so forth.

Finally, there are differences in ratings between corporates and municipals. Two stand out.

In the first place, a sizable minority of municipal bonds are not rated at all. Although this can be a danger sign, it is not invariably so. A municipality may not have enough debt outstanding to warrant a rating. Or it may not have applied for a rating. Or it may have issued so-called revenue bonds, whose payments of principal and interest are dependent upon the revenue they generate from a particular project, such as a sports arena. The investment advisory organizations occasionally do not rate revenue bonds until the related facilities have had some operating experience.

In the second place, there are certain fine differences in the way municipal bonds are rated. Fitch and Standard & Poor's use the same symbols that they use for corporate bonds. Moody's does, too, but in two cases it adds a refinement.

The refinement involves bonds rated A and Baa—or A and BBB as Fitch and Standard & Poor's would put it. To certain bonds in these two categories, Moody's adds the number one to the letter ratings. Thus the bonds may be given ratings of A-1 or Baa-1.

Such a rating merely indicates that the bonds are somewhat safer than other bonds in their categories, but not quite safe enough to warrant a higher rating. Thus, in essence, a bond rated A-1 falls between one rated Aa and one rated A.

Moody's found these special ratings necessary because of the huge number of bonds in the A and Baa categories. There are so many it decided it had to make some distinction among them.

So much for the differences between municipals and corporates. As you can see, the most important are that municipals provide tax-exempt income and are usually issued in serial form.*

Within this broad framework, municipals break into six general categories. These categories reflect the sources of revenue that stand behind the bonds' expected principal and interest payments.

First come *general obligation bonds.* They are backed by the full faith, credit and taxing power of the issuer. In other words, the issuer promises to use its full tax power to ensure that principal and interest are paid on time.

General obligation bonds are the most common of all municipals and also have the strongest backing. For this reason they tend to receive the highest credit ratings and return the lowest yields.

Generally holders of these bonds have first claim on a state's or city's revenues. Yet over the years the question has sometimes arisen whether such bondholders could actually exert such a claim in case of default. As the question is often put: Would a city really pay interest to its bondholders before it paid salaries to its policemen?

Court cases have been extremely limited and the decisions somewhat conflicting. But the question is something of an abstraction. Very few municipal bonds, let alone general obligation bonds, enter default, although New York City's recent near defaults provide food for thought.

Second come *limited-tax, general obligation bonds.* These bonds are identical with general obligations in all but one respect. There is some limit on the tax power that the issuer will exert to pay principal and interest.

---

*Those few municipals issued in term form are known in the trade as *dollar bonds* because they are quoted in terms of their prices rather than their yields.

For example, the issuer may limit the rate at which it will levy property taxes. Or it may set aside only a certain stipulated amount of these taxes.

(3) Third come *special-tax bonds*. These bonds are not secured by the full faith, credit and taxing power of the issuer, but by some special tax. For example, they may be secured by a tax on gasoline or a tax on tobacco products.

(4) Fourth come *revenue bonds*. These bonds are secured only by the earnings of the facility that was constructed from the proceeds from the bonds' sale. This may be an airport, an electric or gas system, a toll bridge, a turnpike or some other facility useful to the general or a specific public.

As a group, revenue bonds are considered less safe than general obligation bonds. This viewpoint is both fair and unfair. Over the years revenue bonds have been in default much more often than general obligation bonds. Even so, their total number of defaults has been small. And some dealers assert that some revenue bonds are superior to some general obligation bonds. So much depends on the revenue generated by a particular facility.

As we learned in Chapter 4, the Chesapeake Bridge and Tunnel Authority's Series C bonds went into default because the facility just didn't attract as many drivers as was expected. Yet similar facilities regularly stash away more than they have to pay in interest. The Delaware Turnpike, for example, is reported to have earned more than twice as much as it must pay in annual interest. And several other turnpikes have done almost as well.

Certain revenue bonds are known as *double-barreled bonds*. This means that they are backed not only by the revenues generated by a particular facility, but also by some other source.

For instance, the New York State Thruway was financed partly from revenue bonds, partly from state-guaranteed bonds. The state promised that if revenues proved insufficient to take care of the interest on both bonds, it would pay the interest on the guaranteed bonds. The revenue bonds would then have first call on the thruway's earnings.

Fifth come *housing authority bonds.* These bonds vary greatly in type. Some are guaranteed by the cities in which the housing authorities' projects are located. Thus they are general obligations of the cities in question. Others are issued by a local Public Housing Authority. But if the rents generated by an authority's projects are insufficient to pay interest, the United States government makes up the difference. Still others are revenue bonds pure and simple.

Obviously, the first two kinds of bonds are considered very safe, almost always receive high credit ratings and pay commensurately lower rates of interest. There is nothing inherently wrong with the straight revenue bonds, but you should be aware of what they are and not be confused merely because the issuer includes the name of its state in its title.

For example, the New York State Housing Finance Agency issues bonds for hospitals, mental institutions and public buildings. Yet its bonds are pure revenue bonds and do not carry the legal backing of New York State.

Finally, there are *industrial revenue* or *industrial development bonds,* which skyrocketed into prominence in the late 1960s. To attract industry, a city or town would float a bond issue and use the proceeds to build a plant or other facility desired by a particular company. The company then took over the facility on a rental basis, and its rental payments were used to pay interest on the bonds.

This kind of deal proved so popular that, in 1968 alone, some $1.6 billion of industrial development bonds were issued. Because the interest was tax-exempt, both the U.S. Treasury and municipalities lost revenue at an alarming rate. So Congress passed the 1968 Revenue & Expenditure

Control Act, limiting this kind of bond to very small issues and very special purposes.

Yet it left one important loophole. The loophole involved bonds whose proceeds are largely used to finance pollution-control facilities. Hence the rise of *pollution-control bonds,* of which you may have read a great deal in recent years. These bonds are revenue bonds of a varying nature.

Take a real-life example of how they work. In 1972 Gulf Oil was faced with the prospect of spending $25 million to reduce pollution at a refinery in Philadelphia. So it persuaded the Philadelphia Authority for Industrial Development, a municipal agency, to float tax-exempt bonds worth that amount. The interest on the bonds was more than two percentage points less than what Gulf would have had to pay if it had issued bonds of its own. Result: the oil company will save nearly $10 million in interest payments over a seventeen-year period.

Furthermore, Gulf became legal owner of the antipollution facilities. As a result, it can enjoy the benefits of the investment tax credit, depreciation and rapid amortization, in addition to paying less interest than it otherwise would.

Pollution-control bonds have become immensely popular in a short period of time. In 1971 some $88 million worth were brought to market. In 1972 another $548 million were offered. In 1973 the figure climbed to about $1.8 billion. As a result, one investment expert estimates that such bonds will account for about 25 percent of all the money industry spends on pollution control throughout this decade.

The reasons for this popularity should be obvious. The bonds offer decided economic advantages to industry, which rarely earns anything from its antipollution efforts. They also offer decided economic advantages to communities, which obtain cleaner air, rivers or whatever at little cost to themselves. Finally, they offer decided advantages to investors, who get a chance to put their money into something with public value that also provides tax-exempt income.

States, cities and so forth issue tax-exempt notes as well as tax-exempt bonds. Indeed, in 1973 the gross volume of such notes exceeded the gross volume of tax-exempt bonds by nearly $2 billion.

Obviously, these notes pay interest, have maturity dates and feature most of the other attributes of corporate notes. Unfortunately, most are sold in minimum denominations of $25,000.

Now let's turn back to the bonds and look more closely at their advantages and disadvantages. As we have seen, their biggest advantage is tax-exempt interest. The greater your income, the more this tax advantage is worth.

For example, let's suppose you are single and have total taxable income of $13,000 a year. You buy a municipal bond that yields 5 percent annually. To get the same after-tax income from a corporate bond, you would have to find one yielding 7.04 percent.

Or suppose you are single and have total taxable income of $26,000, on which, of course, you pay taxes at a much higher rate. You also buy a municipal bond yielding 5 percent. To get the same after-tax income from a corporate bond, you would have to find one yielding 8.33 percent.

And so on right up the line. If your income is $39,000 a year, you would have to find a corporate bond yielding 11.11 percent to get the same after-tax income you would get from a tax-exempt bond yielding 5 percent. And if your income is $52,000, you would have to find a corporate yielding a whopping 13.16 percent.

What if you are married and file joint returns? The same rule applies. The more you earn, the more sense it makes to own municipal bonds.

For example, if your joint taxable income is $20,000 annually, you would have to find a corporate bond returning 7.35 percent to achieve the after-tax income provided by a tax-exempt returning 5 percent. And if your income is $40,000, you would have to find a corporate returning 9.62 percent.

You'll find the relation between the yields on tax-exempt bonds and the yields on taxable securities clearly spelled out in the chart on the ensuing two pages. Bear in mind that the differences apply not only to corporate bonds, but also to United States government bonds, savings bank deposits and other kinds of fixed-income investments.

You may find the chart on pages 104 and 105 even more illuminating. It has been prepared by Lebenthal & Co., a well-known dealer in municipal bonds. Here is how to use it:

Find your income bracket in column A and then read across the page. For example, a husband and wife who have a joint taxable income of $25,000 after deductions and adjustments are in the 36 percent income tax bracket and must turn over to the federal government thirty-six cents of the next $1 they earn in taxable income. They may keep all of the income generated by a municipal bond paying 5.75 percent (column C). But they can keep only 4.32 percent of the interest from a savings account returning 6.75 percent (column D), only 4.96 percent from a United States government obligation paying 7.75 percent (column E), and only 5.28 percent from a corporate bond paying 8.25 percent (column F). The final column (G) is especially interesting because it shows what a taxable investment would have to pay to match the return from a tax-free 5.75 municipal bond.

Offhand, it may seem as if municipal bonds were just the thing for you. Yet they may not be. Most investment

TAX FREE VS.

This table gives the approximate yields that taxable securities must earn in various income brackets to produce, after tax, yields equal to those on tax-free bonds yielding from 5 to 6.9 percent. The table is computed on the theory that

JOINT RETURN (Taxable income in thousands)	$8 to $12	$12 to $16	$16 to $20	$20 to $24	$24 to $28	$28 to $32	$32 to $36	$36 to $40
TAX BRACKET BY PERCENTAGE	22	25	28	32	36	39	42	45
5.00%	6.41	6.67	6.94	7.35	7.81	8.20	8.62	9.09
5.10	6.54	6.80	7.08	7.50	7.97	8.36	8.79	9.27
5.20	6.67	6.93	7.22	7.65	8.13	8.52	8.97	9.45
5.30	6.79	7.07	7.36	7.79	8.28	8.69	9.14	9.64
5.40	6.92	7.20	7.50	7.94	8.44	8.85	9.31	9.82
5.50	7.05	7.33	7.64	8.09	8.59	9.02	9.48	10.00
5.60	7.18	7.47	7.78	8.24	8.75	9.18	9.66	10.18
5.70	7.31	7.60	7.92	8.38	8.91	9.34	9.83	10.36
5.80	7.44	7.73	8.06	8.53	9.06	9.51	10.00	10.55
5.90	7.56	7.87	8.19	8.68	9.22	9.67	10.17	10.73
6.00	7.69	8.00	8.33	8.82	9.38	9.84	10.34	10.91
6.10	7.82	8.13	8.47	8.97	9.53	10.00	10.52	11.09
6.20	7.95	8.27	8.61	9.12	9.69	10.16	10.69	11.27
6.30	8.08	8.40	8.75	9.26	9.84	10.33	10.86	11.45
6.40	8.21	8.53	8.89	9.41	10.00	10.49	11.03	11.64
6.50	8.33	8.67	9.03	9.56	10.16	10.66	11.21	11.82
6.60	8.46	8.80	9.17	9.71	10.31	10.82	11.38	12.00
6.70	8.59	8.93	9.31	9.85	10.47	10.98	11.55	12.18
6.80	8.72	9.07	9.44	10.00	10.63	11.15	11.72	12.36
6.90	8.85	9.20	9.58	10.15	10.78	11.31	11.90	12.55

TAX EXEMPT YIELD

TAXABLE INCOME

the taxpayer's highest bracket tax rate is applicable to the entire amount of any increase or decrease in his taxable income resulting from a switch from taxable to tax-free securities, or vice versa.

© MERRILL LYNCH, PIERCE, FENNER & SMITH INC.

$40 to $44	$44 to $52	$52 to $64	$64 to $76	$76 to $88	$88 to $100	$100 to $120	$120 to $140	$140 to $160
48	50	53	55	58	60	62	64	66
9.62	10.00	10.64	11.11	11.90	12.50	13.16	13.89	14.71
9.81	10.20	10.85	11.33	12.14	12.75	13.42	14.17	15.00
10.00	10.40	11.06	11.56	12.38	13.00	13.68	14.44	15.29
10.19	10.60	11.28	11.78	12.62	13.25	13.95	14.72	15.59
10.38	10.80	11.49	12.00	12.86	13.50	14.21	15.00	15.88
10.58	11.00	11.70	12.22	13.10	13.75	14.47	15.28	16.18
10.77	11.20	11.91	12.44	13.33	14.00	14.74	15.56	16.47
10.96	11.40	12.13	12.67	13.57	14.25	15.00	15.83	16.76
11.15	11.60	12.34	12.89	13.81	14.50	15.26	16.11	17.06
11.35	11.80	12.55	13.11	14.05	14.75	15.53	16.39	17.35
11.54	12.00	12.77	13.33	14.29	15.00	15.79	16.67	17.65
11.73	12.20	12.98	13.56	14.52	15.25	16.05	16.94	17.94
11.92	12.40	13.19	13.78	14.76	15.50	16.32	17.22	18.24
12.12	12.60	13.40	14.00	15.00	15.75	16.58	17.50	18.53
12.31	12.80	13.62	14.22	15.24	16.00	16.84	17.78	18.82
12.50	13.00	13.83	14.44	15.48	16.25	17.11	18.06	19.12
12.69	13.20	14.04	14.67	15.71	16.50	17.37	18.33	19.41
12.88	13.40	14.26	14.89	15.95	16.75	17.63	18.61	19.71
13.08	13.60	14.47	15.11	16.19	17.00	17.89	18.89	20.00
13.27	13.80	14.68	15.33	16.43	17.25	18.16	19.17	20.29

counselors would argue that if you are married and file joint tax returns, you should at least be in the 32 percent tax bracket before you even consider municipals. This means you should have a joint taxable income after adjustments and deductions of at least $20,000. Many counselors, in fact, would place the minimum considerably higher, perhaps at the 48 percent level, in which case you should have a joint taxable income of $40,000.

The reason is simple. Unless you are retired or for some other reason are interested only in income, you should seek some growth in the value of your investments. The chances of obtaining such growth from municipal bonds are limited. Income from a tax-exempt bond equivalent to a 10 percent return from a taxable bond may sound intriguing until you consider that a prudent investor may obtain that much or more, in capital appreciation and dividends, by investing in common stocks.

This doesn't mean that tax-exempts never provide a chance for capital gains. You can buy such bonds at deep discounts, just as you can buy corporates at deep discounts.

For example, as this is written, Lebenthal is offering some New York City bonds paying 2.5 percent interest and due to mature in 1981. The price on the bonds is 75½, and they yield 6.60 percent to maturity. After allowing for the capital gains tax, Lebenthal figures that an investor's total return, in interest and capital gains, will amount to 47.4 percent.

Of course, this return has to be divided by seven years, and that means that it amounts to less than 7 percent a year. Even allowing for taxes, you may do as well in the stock market. But again you may not. It's a case of betting on a virtually sure thing versus a mere possibility.

As we have seen, the municipal bond market also offers infinite choice. And it is growing all the time. In 1973 there was some $23 billion in tax-exempt bond financing. By

1980 it's believed the volume may reach $30 billion annually.

But if you decide to buy municipals, bear these tips in mind:

- Look first at bonds issued by your own state or one of its authorities or municipalities. By buying such bonds, you'll probably avoid state and local taxes.

- Check a bond's marketability before you buy it. Good municipals with good ratings are easily salable. But remember that the municipal bond market is always a buyer's market. The price you get will be determined by the best available bid. And if you are trying to unload $15,000 worth of bonds, the typical dealer will not spend as much time seeking the best bid as he would if you were an institution trying to unload $1.5 million worth.

- Buy into large issues. When a municipality puts out a really sizable issue, it must usually offer a higher yield than would normally be required to attract investors. So you'll get a higher rate. And if you should have to sell the bond before maturity, you'll probably get a better price than you would if you tried to unload a bond from a small issue.

- Buy municipals for the long term and hold onto them if you possibly can. If you're not absolutely certain you can keep your money invested for twenty years or more, buy serial municipals with short maturities.

- Make sure that any bond you buy has a legal opinion printed on it or attached to it, indicating that the bond is legally valid. These opinions are usually included as a matter of course. A bond without one is not considered a valid delivery.

Historically, the major danger to buying municipals has lain in the possibility that they would suffer a decline in market value. The next greatest danger has lain in the possibility of default. Fortunately, the latter danger has not been great.

Even during the Great Depression, less than 2 percent of the average of state and local debt was in default at any one time. And in most cases, municipal bondholders were paid off within a few years. Permanent losses during the

A	B	C	D
If your net taxable income is	Your federal tax bracket is	Your take-home from a tax-free 5.75 percent bond is	Your take-home from a bank paying 6.75 percent is
$16,000	28 percent	5.75 percent	4.86 percent
$25,000	36 percent	5.75 percent	4.32 percent
$35,000	42 percent	5.75 percent	3.92 percent
$50,000	50 percent	5.75 percent	3.38 percent
$75,000	55 percent	5.75 percent	3.04 percent
$100,000	62 percent	5.75 percent	2.57 percent

1929–37 period amounted to less than one-half of 1 percent of the average debt outstanding.

The record since World War II has been even better. Defaults have been relatively few. And the overwhelming majority have involved unrated bonds.

Of course, the past is an indicator, but not a guarantee, of the future. But if you want additional protection, you can now buy insurance against defaults. MGIC Investment Corporation is offering such on portfolios worth $50,000 or

E	**F**	**G**
Your take-home from a U.S. government bond paying 7.75 percent is	Your take-home from a corporate bond paying 8.25 percent is	To keep 5.75 percent from a taxable bond, you would have to receive
5.58 percent	5.94 percent	7.99 percent
4.96 percent	5.28 percent	8.98 percent
4.50 percent	4.79 percent	9.91 percent
3.88 percent	4.13 percent	11.50 percent
3.49 percent	3.71 percent	12.78 percent
2.95 percent	3.14 percent	15.13 percent

more. Premiums vary according to the portfolio's face value, but do not exceed 0.35 percent annually.

What are the most important things we have learned from this chapter? We have learned that municipal bonds are issued by states, cities and public bodies on the state and local level. We have learned that the bonds are sometimes guaranteed by the full legal and tax power of a state or city and sometimes not. We have learned that the interest from them is exempt from federal taxation and sometimes from state and city taxation as well, making it much more valuable than an equivalent amount of interest from corporate bonds and other fixed-income investments. We have learned that the bonds are commonly issued in serial form, making it easy for an investor to invest so as to get his principal back precisely when he wants it. But we have also learned that the wealthier you are, the more valuable the income from them is and that you should probably not invest in them at all unless tax-free income is of some importance to you. Finally, we have learned that fraud has crept into the industry to a small, but noticeable, degree and that you should be cautious about what municipal bond houses you deal with.

Chapter 8

"plethora" - excess or surplus.

U.S. Treasury Securities: A Plethora of Issues

When people talk about government securities, they are not referring to the savings bonds you may have purchased during World War II or some subsequent period. Rather they are referring to four other types of securities periodically issued by the U.S. Treasury. These securities are known as *bills, certificates* or certificates of indebtedness, *notes* and *bonds*.

What are their attractions?

First, they provide maximum safety of principal. In fact, there simply are no safer investments. That's because they are backed by the full faith, authority and taxing power of the United States government itself. If the government ever defaulted on payment of principal or interest, the country would be in very serious condition, both nationally and internationally. Indeed, our entire economic structure might be in jeopardy, and it is likely that many municipal and corporate bonds would also be in arrears.

Second, they are highly liquid. If you should have to sell a government security before it matures, you would almost invariably find a ready market for it. And the risk that its price would have fallen substantially below the price you paid for it would be somewhat less than it would be in relation to other kinds of bonds.

Among other reasons: the securities are considered even safer than top-rated corporate bonds. And as you know, the prices of these bonds vary only in relation to interest rates, not economic conditions.

Third, government securities often offer attractive yields to persons interested in current income. Because these securities are the safest of all investments, the yields on them are never quite so high as those on corporate bonds. Even so, the difference is sometimes very narrow.

Ordinarily, the difference ranges from as little as one-third of one percentage point to something in excess of two points. The spread tends to widen when investors become unusually concerned about safety of principal, as they did when the Penn Central Railroad went bankrupt a few years ago, or when there is an unusually large supply of government issues or an unusually small supply of corporates.

Finally, the interest from government securities is, to some extent, tax-exempt. Specifically it is exempt from all state and local income taxes, although not from estate and gift taxes imposed at these levels nor from federal income, estate and gift taxes.

Safety of principal. Unusual liquidity. Attractive yields. Limited taxation. These are the chief virtues of government securities. There are still others, as we will see later on. But first let's study the nature of the securities themselves.

First come the *bills*. Each week the Treasury issues two sets of bills—one maturing in 91 days, the other in 182 days or six months. And each month it issues two other sets—

one maturing in nine months, the other in a few days less than one year. All of the issues are designed to provide the government with quick and ready cash.

None pay a stated rate of interest. Rather they are sold, both initially and subsequently, at discounts from their face values. Thus the buyer's yield or rate of return represents the difference between what he pays for a bill and what he receives when he redeems it, plus, of course, the period of time for which it is outstanding.

For example, suppose a $10,000 91-day note were selling for $9,800 or $98 of each $100 of its face value. The rate of return would be determined by dividing the discount by the bill's face value and expressing the resulting percentage (.02) as an annual rate, using a 360-day year. Thus:

$$\frac{100-98}{100} \times \frac{360}{91} = 7.91 \text{ percent}$$

The yield on these bills is largely determined by the law of supply and demand. The bills are very popular with institutional investors, and they usually fix the yield by means of competitive bidding.

Individuals, however, usually bid for the bills on a noncompetitive basis. If you were to do so, you would agree to pay the average price of the bids that the Treasury accepts from institutional investors. This would be much to your advantage because it would mean that you would be able to obtain at least some of the bills, yet not have to outbid others in order to get them.

You may buy such bills through a broker or your commercial bank. If you are an important customer, a bank may charge you nothing for the service. If you are not an important customer, it may charge you anywhere from a few dollars to $25, which will, of course, reduce your yield from the bills.

Better yet, when the bills are first issued, you can buy

them from one of the nation's twelve Federal Reserve Banks or their thirty-six branches, either by mail or in person. The Federal Reserve Banks and branches make no charge of any kind on either purchase or redemption.

A fact sheet on how to make such purchases—or tenders, as they are known—is available from the banks themselves or from the Bureau of Public Debt, Department of the Treasury, Washington, D.C. 20220. Basically, all that's involved is writing a certified personal check or a cashier's check payable to the Federal Reserve Bank for the full face value of the bill you wish to purchase.

Once the discount rate is established, the Federal Reserve Bank will refund the difference between what you paid and what the bills actually sold for and forward you a certificate of ownership, using registered mail and insuring the certificate at the Treasury's expense. When the issue matures, of course, you must redeem the bill or use it toward purchase of a new one.

If you want to buy a bill after its initial issuance or to sell one before its maturity, you can always do so in the active secondary market. But because the bills are outstanding for such short periods of time, there is usually little point in doing so except in an emergency. You will only have to pay bank or broker fees, as the Federal Reserve Banks do not maintain a secondary market in the issues.

In addition to being cost-free when they are purchased from a Federal Reserve Bank, the bills possess all of the advantages of government securities cited earlier, plus a rather special one of their own: they are often considered a very good place to put one's money during periods of stock market uncertainty.

If the market seems unstable, you can sit on the sidelines for a few months until the situation becomes clarified. All the while, you will receive some return on your money.

It's amusing to note that the Lady Luck Casino in Las

Vegas, Nevada, was recently reported to have invested all of its employees' profit-sharing fund in Treasury bills. The casino's president explained that investing in stocks represented too much of a gamble. He said he'd rather shoot craps.

Despite all their advantages, Treasury bills also suffer from drawbacks. First and foremost, the yields on them fluctuate frequently and sometimes sharply. This means that they are a much better buy at certain times than at others.

For example, at the tip end of April 1974 newly issued 91-day bills were yielding almost 8.91 percent. About a month earlier, such bills were yielding 8.30 percent, a month before that 7.18 percent, a year earlier 6.25 percent and back in 1967 an average of 4.32 percent.

Because the yield often fluctuates so sharply, it is always wise to compare it with the interest payable on ordinary savings accounts that can be quickly withdrawn without penalty. Sometimes the bills yield considerably more than ordinary savings accounts, sometimes not as much. But when they yield less, it is well to bear in mind that the income is exempt from state and local income taxes, while the interest from savings accounts is not. This factor may more than make up the difference.

Another disadvantage to Treasury bills lies in the fact that they can be purchased only in minimum denominations of $10,000 and further multiples of $5,000. At one time they were available in denominations of $1,000. But a few years ago they became so popular that the cost of the paperwork involved in processing small bills became exorbitant. Hence the change.

Finally, all Treasury bills are issued in bearer form. This makes them fine collateral for loans. But it also means they are easily subject to theft.

Treasury *certificates* pay a fixed rate of interest, carry

maturities of no more than one year and are available only in bearer form. In recent years, however, the government has refrained from issuing certificates, and as of a recent date none were outstanding. Reason: the money can be raised more conveniently by means of bills.

Treasury _notes_ also return a fixed rate of interest, payable semiannually. They carry maturities of not less than one year nor more than seven years. The longer the maturity, the greater the interest usually is.

In May 1974 the Treasury issued two sets of notes, worth a total of $3.75 billion and due to mature in 1976 and 1978 respectively. Both sets offered interest of 8.75 percent annually. This was the highest interest rate on this kind of security in the country's history.

Then, in August 1974 it offered two more sets of notes, worth a total of $4 billion, and due to mature in 1977 and 1980 respectively. These notes provide annual interest of 9 percent.

As you can guess, the notes can be bought for more or less than their face value. So their yields may be more or less than their stated rates of interest.

Like Treasury bills, the notes may be purchased on a noncompetitive basis from Federal Reserve Banks at no charge. Or they can be bought through certain commercial banks or brokerage houses for a fee.

They possess three distinct advantages over bills. Because they are outstanding for longer periods of time, they normally return more interest. They are usually available in denominations as small as $1,000, the May issue cited above being a notable exception. And most can be purchased in either registered or bearer form.

Treasury _bonds_ have all the features of other kinds of bonds, such as fixed rates of interest and fixed maturities. They are issued for at least five years and usually for seven or more. Some, although not all, are subject to call.

In recent years, however, these bonds have had a curious history. The fact is, the government has issued relatively few of them. Between 1965 and 1971, it didn't issue any at all.

The reason is simple. Some years ago Congress forbad the government to pay interest of more than 4.25 percent on bonds. That rate hasn't been competitive for some time. As a result, the Treasury has had to issue more and more debt in the form of short-term bills.

This has left it in an awkward position. On the one hand, it doesn't like paying the high rate of interest that has recently prevailed on long-term securities, any more than any corporation or municipality does. On the other hand, it doesn't like so much of its debt to be in the form of short-term securities that have to be rolled over every few months.

In 1971, however, Congress amended the law, allowing the Treasury to issue up to $10 billion in long-term bonds at rates above the legal ceiling, and two years later it gave permission for another $5 billion to be issued in this fashion. As a result, the Treasury has entered the long-term bond market considerably more often.

For example, in May 1974 it sold nearly $2 billion worth of twenty-five-year bonds, paying 8.5 percent interest. This was the highest rate paid on such securities in history, even higher than the 8 percent that was offered on $6.5 million worth of bonds sold in 1799 and 1800, when the government sought "millions for defense, but not one cent for tribute."

Government bonds possess all the basic virtues of other government securities. In addition, they are usually available in denominations of as little as $1,000 and can be bought in either registered or bearer form. Like bills, they can be obtained directly from Federal Reserve Banks when first issued. Or they can be bought from the Office of the

Treasurer of the United States, Securities Division, Washington, D.C. 20220. In either case, there is no charge.

In recent years government securities have traded in the over-the-counter market. But in 1974 the New York Stock Exchange announced that it would list all federal bonds and notes, except foreign series. So they are now traded both places, although the overwhelming majority of trading is still done in the over-the-counter market.

You learned in Chapter 2 what government listings look like. Only two further points need clarification.

Sometimes a government bond's maturity date is listed in hyphenated fashion—e.g., 94-86. This merely means that the bonds will mature in 1994 but can be called in as early as 1986.

Also, quotations of government bond prices often include percentages that reflect their yields to maturity. These yields, of course, include not only the interest that the bonds return but also the capital gains or losses, if any, that will be realized when they mature.

Yields to maturity provide a convenient way of comparing bonds. But bear in mind that bonds with identical yields may not be equally good buys. One may be selling at a much greater discount than the other. As a result, a larger part of its yield to maturity will represent potential capital gain. Naturally, this gain will be taxed at a lower rate than the interest will.

Obviously, it is possible to buy government bonds on margin. Often, in fact, the margin required by brokerage houses does not exceed 10 percent, which is considerably less than that required on corporate bonds and stocks.

As a result, it is very easy to speculate in governments. As we saw in Chapter 4, both the potential rewards and risks are very great. But speculation like this is for the hardy with money they can afford to lose. So many factors impinge on the movements of long-term interest rates that it is even difficult for professionals to be sure whether they will rise or fall—and by how much.

There's one other kind of government bond in which you may be interested. Because it's suggestive of funerals, it's known as a *flower bond.*

Flower bonds are usually available at less than their face values. And if they are in their owners' estates at the time of death, they may be redeemed at their face values to pay estate taxes, no matter what prices they are currently selling at.

The bonds will be valued at their face values to help determine the size of the owner's estate. And these values will, of course, have some effect on the amount of *estate* taxes due. But there will be no *income* or *capital gains* taxes due on the difference between the bonds' market and face values.

If these bonds interest you, it's worth mentioning that they will not be around forever. The last new issue came out in the 1960s, Congress has forbad the issuance of any more, and those still outstanding are being retired at the rate of $1 billion or so a year.

You can obtain a free list of those still available directly from the government. Write the Bureau of the Public Debt, Department of the Treasury, Washington, D.C. 20220.

Now let's turn to those old favorites—savings bonds. As you probably know, they come in two forms. The better known are called Series E bonds. The others are known as Series H bonds.

Millions of Americans have purchased both kinds over the years. But, except in time of war, they may not have been wise to do so. Although the bonds are considered very safe investments, the return on them has never been especially good.

Fortunately, the situation has improved. Late in 1973 the government increased the effective rate of interest to 6 percent annually. That may not be an eye-opening figure, but at least it's better than the interest that is paid on many ordinary savings accounts.

The Series E bonds are sold in seven denominations ranging in face value from $25 to $1,000. Since the bonds are sold at a 25 percent discount from these face values, a $25 bond costs $18.75 and a $1,000 bonds costs $750.

The difference between these purchase prices and the bonds' face values when they mature is, in effect, the interest as if such had been compounded semiannually. At the present time, the bonds mature in five years and, as noted, return 6 percent. They cannot be called in.

No individual may buy more than $5,000 worth of the bonds in any one year. But two individuals, such as a husband and wife, may jointly purchase $10,000 worth.

The bonds are available only in registered form and may be bought and redeemed through the Office of the Treasurer of the United States, Federal Reserve Banks and their branches, or ordinary commercial banks, at no charge. Furthermore, any one of these sources will replace any bonds that have been lost, stolen or destroyed without argument.

In addition, the bonds are free from taxes at the state and local level, although not from other kinds of taxes at these levels nor from federal income, estate or gift taxes. Yet a clever investor may escape taxes altogether—and in very legal fashion.

For example, suppose a father wants to establish a college-education fund for one of his children. To this end, he buys a $1,000 bond each and every year and registers it in the child's name.

The first year, he has the youngster file an income tax return, reporting the interest that has accrued on the bonds. Because the child is apt to be in a very low income bracket, he will probably not have to pay any income taxes on this interest.

The father keeps a copy of the return. Unless the youngster's income status changes, he will not have to file further returns. The initial return will establish proof of the father's intent to establish an education fund. When the bonds mature, the youngster will be able to cash them in tax-free because he has, in effect, been reporting the income on them each and every year they have been outstanding.

Despite their virtues, E bonds suffer from drawbacks. The owner cannot sell them, give them away or use them as collateral for a loan. He will obtain the full rate of effective interest only if he holds them until maturity. And although this rate has risen steadily from 2.9 percent in World War II to the 6 percent prevailing today, it has rarely, if ever, been fully competitive with that available from many other fixed-income securities.

For just this reason, some investment counselors think E bonds should be purchased only if the owner wishes to express patriotism or set up or join an enforced savings program. Perhaps this criticism is too harsh. Nonetheless, it is doubtful whether E bonds should form the backbone of anyone's investment portfolio.

Series H bonds are sold in denominations of $500, $1,000 and $5,000 and may be bought from the same sources as E bonds, at no charge. Unlike E bonds, however, they are purchasable at their face values, and they return regular interest, which is payable semiannually.

The amount of this interest rises over the life of the bonds. But if they are held to maturity, ten years later, the interest will average out to 6 percent annually. If cashed in early, it will be less.

The bonds enjoy the same basic advantages and suffer from the same basic drawbacks as E bonds. Thus they are considered very safe and convenient, are available only in registered form and cannot be called in. Furthermore, they are not subject to state and local income taxes.

On the other hand, they cannot be sold, given away or used as collateral. Only $5,000 of them may be purchased by any one individual in any one year. And the return on them is not as good as that from certain other investments.

But mark this: there is a way to combine the purchase of E and H bonds and avoid virtually all federal taxation during one's lifetime. The idea may have particular appeal to people who want to establish retirement funds. It can be implemented as follows:

Over a period of years, buy as many E bonds as you wish, up to the $5,000 annual maximum, and hold onto them past their maturities. They will continue to earn interest at the 6 percent annual rate. But you can defer paying taxes on this interest until you cash the bonds in.

But don't cash them in. When you get ready to retire, exchange them for H bonds worth the same amount. By government fiat, the $5,000 annual limitation on purchase of H bonds will be waived. And you will still not have to pay any taxes on the interest from the E bonds.

You will, however, have to pay taxes on the interest you receive from the H bonds. And you will also have to pay taxes on the E bonds when you cash in the H bonds or when the latter mature. But these maturities are often extended. So you may end up paying no taxes on the E bonds at all, in which case they will be taxable only to your estate.

But before exchanging E bonds for H bonds, you will want to investigate one possible pitfall. Depending somewhat on how long you have held the E bonds, you may find the interest from them is greater than it would be from H bonds, particularly in the first year that you would own the H bonds. If current income will be very important to you, you ought to weigh this danger carefully.

Finally, the government issues U.S. Retirement Plan Bonds, which are available for purchase only in connection with bond-purchase plans and pension- and profit-sharing plans set up under the Self-employed Individuals Tax Retirement Act. Under this Act, qualified individuals may set aside either 15 percent of their income or $7,500 yearly, whichever is less, toward retirement. These funds may, of course, be invested in retirement bonds.

The bonds are issued in various denominations ranging from $50 to $1,000. Their chief asset lies in the fact that like all government issues, they are considered among the safest investments in the world.

Among their drawbacks: They may be redeemed only when the owner dies, becomes disabled or reaches 59½ years of age. Their interest is payable only upon redemption. And this interest tends to be less than that which is available on other corporate and government securities.

To sum up this chapter, we have learned that the U.S. Treasury issues four kinds of securities—bills, certificates, notes and bonds—plus two kinds of savings bonds, and retirement bonds. We have learned that all these issues are very popular with investors and are considered as safe as any investment.

On the negative side, we have ascertained that although the yields on certain government issues sometimes come very close to matching those available on other comparable fixed-income securities, they rarely close the gap. Last but not least, we must not forget that, except when they are successfully bought and sold for speculative purposes, Treasury issues provide somewhat limited protection against inflation. This, of course, is a drawback inherent to virtually all fixed-income securities.

End of Chpt. 8

Chapter 9

Agency Issues: Uncle Sam's Attractive Nephews

The U. S. Treasury is not the only branch of the federal government that issues bonds and notes. A dozen or more other agencies do so, too. Not unnaturally, their securities are known as *agency issues* or just as agencies.

In recent years the market in these issues has grown remarkably. According to Salomon Brothers, the net increase in privately held federal agency debt amounted to $4.8 billion in 1966. In the ensuing five years there were still further increases, some larger, some smaller. Then in 1972 came a record increase of $9.2 billion. And as if that weren't enough, the figure jumped an astounding $21 billion in the following year.

The best known of the agencies that issue debt securities are, in alphabetical order:

- The District Banks for Cooperatives, which make short-term and intermediate-term loans to farm cooperatives that market agricultural products.

- The Export-Import Bank, which makes loans to American and foreign firms in an effort to beef up foreign trade.

- The Farmers Home Administration, which makes loans to individual farmers to buy, build or enlarge houses, to buy land and to achieve other, similar purposes.

- The Federal Home Loan Banks, which serve as a reserve credit agency and lender to thousands of savings and loan associations and other thrift institutions that make mortgage loans to homeowners.

- The Federal Home Loan Mortgage Corporation, which buys mortgages from Federal Home Loan Banks and other financial institutions and sells them to interested investors.

- The Federal Intermediate Credit Banks, which serve somewhat the same function as the Banks for Cooperatives, lending to various credit associations that in turn make loans to farmers.

- The Federal Land Banks, which are a source of long-term credit to various associations that make loans to farmers to purchase farm machinery, livestock and land.

- The Federal National Mortgage Association, more popularly known as Fannie Mae, which performs various functions in the mortgage market, such as buying mortgages insured and guaranteed by other government agencies, then reselling them to institutions and individuals interested in this kind of investment.

- The Government National Mortgage Association, commonly referred to as Ginnie Mae, which guarantees mortgages that have been issued by banks and other institutions and that have also been endorsed by one or another of various government agencies.

- The Inter-American Development Bank, which makes development loans in Latin and South America.*

- The International Bank for Reconstruction and Development, widely referred to as the World Bank, which makes many of its loans to governments and private organizations in underdeveloped countries.*

- The Tennessee Valley Authority, which sometimes borrows funds to finance its power plants.

Most of the issues of these agencies are much like other bonds and notes. They have face values, pay stated rates of interests and mature on certain stated dates. On the other hand, only occasionally can they be called in ahead of maturity.

We won't examine all these agency issues. It would be confusing to try to remember all the details. Besides, information about the issues is readily available from most brokers and bond dealers.

Instead we will look in some detail at the issues of the two agencies that are perhaps the most popular of the group. Before doing so, let's see how the agency issues stack up against the various securities issued by the U.S. Treasury.

Agency issues are not considered quite as safe as those issued by the Treasury. Reason: although a few of the issues carry the full backing of the United States government,

*Strictly speaking, this is an international organization, comprised of many nations. But its issues are treated as government agency issues.

most do not. Instead they are backed only by the agencies that issue them.

In actual practice, this makes little difference to the safety of the investor's principal. No agency has ever defaulted on its issues.

The fact is, the United States government would be very embarrassed if one of its agencies did default and would probably take some kind of remedial action. Some evidence: during the Great Depression, the Treasury went to the aid of the Federal Land Banks when many farmers' mortgages were foreclosed.

But the government is not usually required to render such aid. And for this reason, most agency issues are considered slightly less safe than Treasury issues.

As a result, they almost always return higher yields than Treasury issues. In recent years the normal difference in yields on issues of comparable maturities has amounted to 12 to 20 basis points or one-eighth to one-fifth of 1 percent.

Sometimes, of course, this difference vanishes. And sometimes it rises to a full percentage point or more. In the latter case, the agency issues are usually considered a clearly better buy.

Although Ginnie Mae pass-through certificates are issued only in registered form, many other agency issues are put out only in bearer form. They thus incur the same dangers as comparable corporate and municipal securities do.

The tax status of the agency issues varies, depending on the agency involved. Ginnie Maes and Fannie Maes are not exempt from state and local income taxes. But many other agency issues are, although they are not, of course, exempt from state and local gift and inheritance taxes nor from all the various taxes imposed by the federal government.

Interestingly, only Farmers Home Administration issues can be bought directly from the agency itself. All the others must be bought differently.

Thus all the agencies have fiscal agents in New York City. Example: the Fiscal Agent of the Federal Land Banks.

When they have an issue to sell, these agencies put together a nationwide sales group and let its members buy the issue at a discount from the listed price. These sales groups usually include banks, brokerage houses and other securities dealers, and the sale of the securities is publicly announced through newspapers and other means.

Each firm that belongs to a sales group accepts orders on the listed terms. If your order is accepted, you will not have to pay a commission. But you may have to pay a service charge, the size of which may vary in accordance with the size of your order. For example, Merrill Lynch, Pierce, Fenner & Smith would charge three-eighths of a point for an order for $5,000 worth of agency bonds, one-quarter of a point for an order for $10,000 worth, one-eighth of a point for an order for $26,000 worth, and one-sixteenth of a point for an order for $50,000 worth. The brokerage house would actually quote you these charges in thirty-seconds of a point because that is how government and agency issues are priced.

Only two other special points need be made about these issues.

First, they come in a wide range of maturities. For example, in the spring of 1974 the Federal Land Banks issued $300 million worth of bonds due to mature in fifteen months, the Export-Import Bank $400 million worth of debentures due to mature in five years, and the Farmers Home Administration $200 million worth of notes due to mature in fifteen years. Issues with both shorter and longer maturities are also frequently available.

Second, agency issues also come in a wide range of minimum denominations. Thus Federal Land Bank issues are available in units of $1,000. Ginnie Mae pass-through certificates, on the other hand, can only be bought in minimum initial units of $25,000. Yet most other agency issues come in minimum denominations of $5,000 or $10,000, and some agencies put out issues of both sizes.

Let's now turn to the issues of the two government agencies that are, if not the most popular, certainly the best known in the country. The first is Fannie Mae, the second Ginnie Mae.

Fannie Mae performs several important functions, probably the most important of which is the purchase and resale of mortgages insured or guaranteed by the Veterans Administration or certain other government agencies. In connection with its various operations, it issues preferred and common stock, short-term discount notes that are similar to commercial paper, so-called participation certificates that represent shares in obligations held by the Department of Housing and Urban Development and other government agencies, plus debentures and notes. For our purposes, the last two are probably of most immediate interest.

The debentures, which are much like corporate debentures, are issued in widely varying maturities ranging up to twenty-five years or more. The big majority, however, have maturities of no more than ten years, and a number mature in much less time than that.

None carry the backing of the United States government. Rather they are backed by the cash, mortgages and other holdings of Fannie Mae.

Most of the issues come in minimum denominations of $10,000. Very occasionally, however, some are issued in minimum denominations of $5,000 or even $1,000. All come in bearer form only.

The yields on the issues tend to be slightly lower than those on Ginnie Maes, but slightly higher than those on

Treasury issues. As noted earlier, the income from them is subject to federal income taxes.

In 1968 Ginnie Mae took over certain of Fannie Mae's functions. In particular, it was ordered to make real estate investment mortgages more attractive to all kinds of investors.

To this end, it backs bonds, participation certificates and so-called pass-through certificates that have been endorsed by various government agencies. The bonds are guaranteed by Ginnie Mae itself and often return good rates of interest. The same is true of the participation certificates.

Yet for a variety of reasons, the pass-throughs are far and away the most popular of the group. Indeed, William W. Bartlett, a vice president of The First Boston Corporation, says they are well on their way to becoming more important than all other agency issues combined.

The pass-through certificates represent shares in pools of mortgages issued by mortgage banks and other institutions and backed by the Federal Housing Administration or the Veterans Administration. Ginnie Mae guarantees *monthly* repayment of both principal and interest, and this guarantee is backed by the full weight of the United States government.

In fact, people who invest in pass-throughs often get their principal back ahead of schedule. This is why the issues are called pass-throughs—repayments above the required level are "passed through" to certificate holders on a pro-rated basis. Such repayments may come about because of mortgage foreclosures or simple prepayments.

Ordinarily, Ginnie Mae-backed mortgages on single-family units run up to thirty years, those on multi-family units up to forty years. But because principal is frequently repaid ahead of schedule, the mortgages have an average life of twelve years in the first instance, twenty in the second. In short, the owner of a Ginnie Mae pass-through can usually expect to receive his total investment back within twelve to twenty years.

The certificates are only available in minimum denominations of $25,000 and further increments of $10,000. But the main drawback to them lies in the possibility of early repayment of their principal. After all, when this happens the investor no longer has his investment.

On the other hand, the investor will have obtained a higher yield than he otherwise would have. Furthermore, early repayments can prove a definite advantage in times of rising interest rates. The investor gets his money back and can invest it more profitably elsewhere.

The securities boast other advantages as well. As noted, they carry the full endorsement of the government and are issued only in registered form. They tend to return higher yields than any other government or agency securities. And these yields are enhanced by the fact that interest is paid monthly rather than semiannually.

What is the precise effect of this payment schedule? If the yield on the pass-throughs is between 6.73 and 7.06 percent, monthly payment of interest will increase the yield another .10 percent on a semiannual basis. If the yield is between 7.07 and 7.39 percent, the monthly payment will increase the yield .11 percent. And so on up the line. If the yield reaches 9.63 percent, the addition will amount to .20 percent.

When you get right down to it, Ginnie Maes offer the best features of both mortgages and government bonds. These include attractive yields, regular cash flow, unusual safety and easy marketability.

The securities can be used for a number of purposes— among others, as retirement funds. Indeed, an investor may well receive a higher rate of return than he would from an annuity.

All in all then, Ginnie Maes may be just the thing for you. At times, however, there may be much to be said for investing in agency issues with terms of five years or even considerably less.

One reason is that in times of climbing interest rates short-term agency issues prove relatively safe. In other words, they are not apt to fall nearly as far in price as long-term corporates and governments are. Also, if you buy short-term agencies when interest rates are not at their highest, you can get your money back as rates begin to rise and invest it elsewhere.

We have learned then that a number of government agencies issue bonds, notes and other kinds of securities that are considered almost as safe as those issued by the Treasury itself. We have also learned that these issues come in a wide range of denominations and maturities, tend to return slightly higher yields than Treasury issues do and are very marketable. Indeed, about the only arguments against agency issues are that most come in bearer form, do not usually yield as much as corporates and, as a general rule, do not enjoy exemption from federal income taxes, as municipals do. This last drawback, of course, is true of virtually all other bonds as well.

As you know, all bond markets have long been dominated by institutional investors. But perhaps nowhere has this been more true than in the market for agency issues. This is too bad because these issues have something to offer to investors interested in bonds.

This is not say that they should necessarily be chosen ahead of corporates, municipals or governments. It is merely to say that investors should be more aware of their availability and merits.

Chapter 10

The Mechanics of Buying and Selling Bonds

So far, I have said very little about how one goes about buying and selling bonds or about what such purchases and sales cost. To be sure, we have learned that it is possible to buy certain Treasury issues from the Treasury itself or from Federal Reserve Banks at no cost. But these purchases are exceptions to the general rule.

It is important that you know something about the mechanics of buying and selling bonds, because the way you go about making such transactions, and the charges that will be imposed on you, can materially reduce the income or profit you hope to achieve. But before looking at these mechanics, let's grasp three basic points about buying and selling bonds.

First, the cost of buying and selling them is usually much lower than the cost of buying and selling stocks. How much lower is difficult to pinpoint because stock commissions are currently in a state of transition. Up until very recent times, they were fixed. As this is written, an increasing number of them are being negotiated. And as of April 1975 all are slated to be negotiated.

At that time, they may go up or down. Or they may do both, depending on the brokerage house that is involved and the size of any given order that it agrees to handle. Yet, whatever happens, it will probably still cost considerably less to buy and sell bonds than it does to buy and sell stocks.

The reasons for this present and probable future state of affairs are varied. For one thing, transactions in bonds usually involve much more money than do those in stocks and, as with so many things in life, the more of anything one buys the cheaper it is apt to be. For another thing, it has historically been easier to execute an order for bonds than it has been to execute an order for stocks. In part, this has been because the great majority of bonds are issued and kept in bearer rather than registered form.

The second point you should understand is the meaning of the term "round lot." If you have ever invested in common stocks, you know perfectly well what the term means. It means 100 shares of any given stock, regardless of the price at which the stock is selling. Anything less than 100 shares is known as an "odd lot."

But when applied to bonds, the term "round lot" has no such clear-cut definition. In using it while talking to individuals, some bondmen mean five bonds with a face value of $5,000. Others mean twenty-five bonds with a face value of $25,000. Many, perhaps most, however, mean 100 bonds with a face value of $100,000.

However they define a round lot, bond dealers all have the same attitude toward it. They would much rather deal in a round lot than in an odd lot.

There are three reasons for this. First, in buying and selling bonds, dealers can prosper only by dealing in big volumes. That's because their profits on small transactions are low. Second, if dealers break up round lots in order to fill orders for odd lots, they may find it difficult to place the bonds that are left over. This is particularly apt to be the case if they approach institutions, which are, after all, their biggest and steadiest customers. Third, dealers know that if they fill an order for an odd lot and the customer later wants to sell, he may have to do so at a price several points below the one prevailing in the market. That's because not many other people may want to buy the odd lot. This, of course, will make the customer unhappy and may even cause him to blame his dealer.

From what has been said so far, you may already have guessed the third basic point you should master. It is not always easy for an individual to place an order for $2,000 or $3,000 or even $5,000 worth of bonds.

Much depends on the individual investment banking firm or brokerage house. Some deal only with institutions. Some do a modest amount of business with individuals. Some do quite a bit of business with individuals, although almost invariably less than they do with institutions.

The First Boston Corporation, for one, deals only with institutions. Says Charles Walsh: "We would handle an order from an individual only in very rare circumstances—if, say, he were the treasurer of a firm that was a very good client of ours. Even then, we would not want to handle an order for five or ten bonds. And if we were willing to handle an order for, say, twenty-five, we would not want to do it very often."

L.F. Rothschild & Co., which is heavily, although not exclusively, oriented toward institutions, would ordinarily require a new client to purchase bonds with a face value of at least $5,000. Other firms like Drexel, Burnham & Co., which deals extensively with both institutions and individuals, would impose a minimum charge of $15 for the purchase of only one or two bonds. This is much more per bond than the purchaser of a round lot would have to pay.

However much business they do with individuals, many firms like L.F. Rothschild and Drexel, Burnham do not actively solicit business from customers who want to invest only a few thousand dollars in bonds. And when they are willing to service such customers, they may do so only after emphasizing the risk involved, in particular the risk that the bonds may be sharply marked down from the prevailing market price if they have to be sold before maturity.

Now how are bonds purchased? As you know, most are sold in the over-the-counter market, which is composed of banks, brokerage houses and other dealers. These various organizations may act either as dealers or as agents.

If they act as dealers, it means that they have underwritten a given bond issue or purchased it for their own inventory. If they act as agents, it means that they do not have a given issue in inventory but must purchase it from another dealer.

Obviously, a dealer who has bonds in inventory has incurred some risk. He has assumed that he will be able to sell the bonds at a profit.

The dealer compensates for this risk by trying to build a profit into the price he charges his customers. Thus he will offer you the bond at a *net price* or on a *net basis*. This price will ordinarily include his profit, the profit representing the difference between what he paid for the bond (what's known as the bid price) and what he is willing to sell it for (the ask price).

Among professionals, this difference is commonly known as *a spread*. You will pay nothing else, except perhaps accrued interest and a postage fee to cover the cost of mailing you the bonds.

The amount of the dealer's spread will vary in accordance with a number of factors, including the nature of the market at any given point in time, the nature of the firm you are dealing with, and the maturity and marketability of the bonds you want to buy or sell.

Two other factors will also play a role. One is the kind of bond you seek—that is, whether it is a corporate, municipal, government or agency bond. The other is the bond's age—that is, whether it is a new or seasoned issue.

The spreads on municipals tend to be the most sizable, those on corporates somewhat less so, and those on governments and agencies less yet. Spreads also tend to be somewhat larger on new issues than seasoned ones.

If the bond were a new municipal, then, as of a recent date, L.F. Rothschild's spread would usually have ranged from about $6 to $15. If the bond were a new corporate, Drexel, Burnham's spread would usually have ranged from about $6 to $12. Spreads on governments and agencies would have been considerably less. As we saw in Chapter 9, Merrill Lynch's spread on a small order would have been only $3.75 per $1,000 bond.

If the issue were seasoned, then the spread would have tended to be smaller, at least on corporates and municipals. In many cases, it would have been about $5 per $1,000 bond, although it could have ranged higher or lower.

You should understand that all spreads may be quoted in points rather than in dollars. In this connection, an eighth of a point is equal to $1.25, a quarter of a point to $2.50, a half a point to $5, three-quarters of a point to $7.50 and a full point to $10.

You should also understand that although a spread is designed to provide a dealer with a profit, he may suffer a loss instead. For example, suppose a dealer makes a successful bid to underwrite a bond issue at its face value (100) and plans to reoffer it to the public at 100.75. This would give him a spread of three-quarters of a point or $7.50 on each bond.

But suppose the issue doesn't sell out. Suppose some remains in his inventory. Suppose interest rates go up, pushing the prices of older bonds down. People may no longer be willing to buy his bonds at 100.75 or even 100. He may have to sell them at a loss, assuming he can sell them at all.

If a dealer does not own the bonds you seek, he must act as an agent, in which case he will probably buy them from another dealer. The other dealer will give him a concession—perhaps $2.50 a bond—and this concession will represent the first dealer's profit. In other words, L.F. Rothschild at least will charge only what you would have to pay the other dealer if you had bought directly from him.

As we have seen, not all bonds are traded in the over-the-counter market. Some are traded on various national or regional exchanges. If you purchase such bonds, their prices will be determined at auction. And you will pay a commission, usually ranging from $2.50 to $10 a bond.

If and when you want to sell your bonds, the dealer will again impose a spread or charge a commission. If the bonds are corporates or municipals, and if you want to sell a reasonable number of them—say, 25—the spread may often be a half point or $5 a bond. But if the bonds aren't very popular—liquid, as bondmen sometimes say—and if you have only two or three of them, the spread may range up to five points or $50.

Enough of spreads and commissions. What you should remember is that they are normally much less than they would be on stocks, that they vary according to the nature of the bond and the condition of the bond market, and that they also vary according to the dealer you are working with. According to Alan W. Leeds, a partner of L.F. Rothschild: "I think you will find there is considerable diversity in the spreads on the purchase and sale of bonds."

In other words, it may pay to shop. This can be particularly important in the case of municipal bonds. Some less reputable houses have been known to impose spreads two or three times as big as the average.

Bear this in mind, too: municipal bonds are almost always issued in bearer form. And L.F. Rothschild's Alan Leeds says he knows of a number of customers who have had their bonds registered after purchase. He says this can be a very costly mistake.

Reason: in registered form, the bonds are nowhere nearly as marketable. As a result, sellers have been known to take losses of up to $700 on $1,000 bonds because the bonds were registered. That's because the potential buyers have wanted them put back in bearer form, which can be a costly business.

How else can you keep your costs down?

Deal only with a very reputable house. Some men in the investment banking business are nowhere nearly as knowledgeable about bonds as they are about stocks. But if they work for a well-regarded house that does any business in bonds at all, it will have a research department on which they can rely for information and guidance.

Don't tie your decision to where you buy solely to the amount of the spread or commission involved. As we have seen, costs can vary. But your main objective should be to buy bonds of good quality.

Have your dealer compute the yield to maturity after all costs have been added. Ordinarily, the price and yield to maturity he quotes you will reflect his spread. But if there are extra costs of any kind, be sure the yield to maturity reflects them, too.

Finally, buy bonds only if you expect to hold them until maturity. In actual practice, it may not always be possible or even wise to do this. But to the extent that you can, you will eliminate selling costs.

The actual placing of an order with a dealer is little

different than placing an order to buy or sell stock. Ordinarily, you can buy a bond by telephone. You can often sell it the same way, although some dealers like to see bonds they sell before making transactions. They say some customers describe their bonds incorrectly over the telephone.

A final word about margins: the Federal Reserve System currently requires that stocks be initially bought at no less than 50 percent margin—that is, that you put up at least that much of the purchase price. The initial margin requirements for bonds are as follows: for corporates, 25 percent of market value; for convertibles, 50 percent of market value; for municipals, 25 percent of market value or 15 percent of face value, whichever is less; and for governments and agencies, 5 percent of face value.

Some brokerage houses may require still higher margins. But they cannot permit lower ones.

As we have seen, you can speculate by buying on margin. But these days, it's an expensive proposition, quite aside from the risk involved. Typically, a brokerage house will charge 1 percent more than the prime rate, which has recently been at or near record levels.

If you do margin, be careful not to margin up to the hilt. Leave yourself a little room for a possible drop in bond prices. That way you won't have to put up extra money at a time when it may be very inconvenient.*

So much for the mechanics of buying and selling bonds. As you can see, costs are relatively low. But they can prove expensive if you buy only one or two bonds that are not

---

*The New York Stock Exchange's *maintenance* margin requirements are currently the same as the Federal Reserve System's *initial* margin requirements, except in the case of stocks and convertible bonds. In the latter two cases, the maintenance requirements are 25 percent rather than 50 percent. This allows for a considerable drop in price before the investor has to put up more money.

widely marketable. Furthermore, you may have to hunt a bit to find a dealer willing to handle a small order.

Is there no way that an investor with only $1,000 to put up can buy bonds easily and inexpensively? Yes, there is. He can buy into a bond fund, and that is the subject of the next chapter.

End of chpt 10

Chapter 11

Bond Funds: Are They Worth the Candle?

If you follow financial news, you have undoubtedly heard or read a great deal about bond funds. Actually, they are nothing new. The well-known Keystone Custodian funds date to 1932, and several others came into existence within the next decade.

But the great boom in bond funds has come about in this decade, as investors have despaired of the stock market and sought refuge in bonds. Indeed, so many funds have come into existence in the last few years that it is difficult to estimate their number. Even so, they total in the hundreds.

These funds have not only proliferated in great numbers, but also in great variety. Indeed, to properly understand them, we must categorize them in three different ways.

First, they must be categorized by their sales charge or lack thereof—that is, as to whether they are *load funds* that levy sales charges on initial purchases, *no-load funds* that levy no such charges, or *closed-end funds* that are sold on commission like common stocks. Second, they must be categorized according to their form of organization—that is, as to whether they are *open-end (mutual) funds, closed-end funds* or *unit trusts.* Finally, they must be categorized by the nature of their holdings—that is, as to whether they invest exclusively or primarily in corporate bonds, convertible bonds, municipal bonds or other kinds of debt securities.

In categorizing bond funds, it is important to avoid a mistake sometimes made in the popular press. We must not lump bond funds together with income funds nor refer to the two kinds of funds as if they were one and the same thing.

Although they are similar in some respects, they also differ. Thus bond funds usually invest all or most of their assets in bonds. Income funds may put a good share of their assets in bonds—typically 35 percent, according to George Putnam, Jr., chairman of the Putnam Management Group, one of the nation's largest mutual fund families. But usually they invest a majority of their assets in preferred and common stocks of a conservative nature.

I do not point this out to denigrate income funds, many of which have proved to be sound investments. I point it out so as to remind you that you should always know exactly what you are buying. In theory, at least, income funds are riskier than bond funds. Yet they also provide more chance for capital gains.

Now let's look more closely at the various categories of bond funds. Bear in mind that all such funds fit not just one, but all three of the categories listed above. Thus a fund may be an open-end load fund specializing in corporate bonds. Or it may be a unit trust, which also charges a load, specializing in municipal bonds.

As we have seen, load funds levy an initial sales charge. In some cases, this charge will run to 8.75 percent of the initial investment, which is comparable to what many mutual stock funds charge. Yet plenty of such funds charge only 4.5 or 3.5 percent, and at least one charges only 1.5 percent.

No-load funds do not levy an initial sales charge. This is because they sell their shares directly to the public rather than through salesmen or brokers. Some load funds say the no-load funds don't provide as much service either, but that may be sales biz.

Like no-load funds, closed-end funds do not levy a sales charge. But you must pay commissions to buy and sell them, just as you would if you were buying and selling stocks.

Whether or not they levy a load, some funds are organized as open-end or mutual funds. Three features distinguish such funds. One, they continually offer new shares to the public and buy back those shares the public wishes to sell. Two, the shares may always be purchased or sold at their net asset value, which is determined by dividing a fund's total net assets by its total number of shares outstanding. Three, the funds regularly buy bonds they consider desirable and sell those they consider undesirable. In short, they seek to increase the overall values of their portfolios as well as return good incomes.

Closed-end funds do not continually offer new shares to the public nor buy those shares back. Once they have made their initial offerings, their shares must be bought and sold in the over-the-counter market, just as individual bonds and stocks are. Furthermore, these shares may be available at either a discount from or premium over their net asset values or real worth. In July 1974 of seventeen closed-end funds regularly listed in *The New York Times,* all but six were selling at discounts. Like the open-end funds, however, the closed-end funds ordinarily do buy and sell bonds from time to time.

Most unit trusts invest in municipal bonds and are commonly sold in individual units worth a certain minimum amount in terms of the face value of their holdings. Almost always this minimum amount is either $1,000 or $5,000, plus a load, plus accrued interest. For example, a municipal investment unit trust recently sponsored by Merrill Lynch, Pierce, Fenner & Smith, Bache & Co. and Reynolds Securities Inc. contains bonds with a total face value of $45 million and is divided into 45,000 units. As a result, the initial offering price, which included a 3.5 percent load and accrued interest, was $1,028.13.

It may seem as if the initial offering price should have been at least $1,035. The reason it was not is that many bonds in the trust were purchased for less than their face value. The 3.5 percent load was then applied to this discounted, rather than the face, value.

Once a trust like this is sold out, that is it. A new investor cannot buy into the trust unless some other investor sells his units back to the trust's sponsors, who usually maintain secondary markets in the units. If the funds don't maintain such markets, owners can only redeem their units through the funds' sponsors.

Even though unit trusts limit their membership, new ones are continually being brought to market. Indeed, some brokerage houses bring out ten or twelve such trusts a year. So if you can't buy into one trust, you can almost certainly buy into another.

One of the principal features of these trusts is that they are not allowed to trade bonds. They may sell the bonds in their portfolios only if the bonds go into default or suffer other setbacks clearly detrimental to the trusts' owners.

As you may have inferred, all these different kinds of bond funds differ from one another in one other important respect. They may or may not require an initial purchase of a certain minimum size.

A very few impose no minimums. A few others require minimums of only $100 or $250. Many, however, insist on minimums of $1,000 or $5,000. Sometimes, although not always, subsequent purchases may be far smaller.

Now, let's look at the funds in accordance with the nature of their holdings:

CORPORATE BOND FUNDS

Obviously, these funds invest all or most of their assets in corporate bonds. As you know, such bonds tend to yield more than other bonds, except perhaps for municipal bonds, whose tax-exempt status puts them in a special category.

It's important to understand, however, that there are corporate bond funds and corporate bond funds. The kind of bonds one fund invests in may be different from the kind another does.

No better example exists than the three Keystone Custodian Bond Funds, The Keystone Building, 99 High Street, Boston, Massachusetts 02104.* All are open-end

*Although I mention certain funds by name in this chapter, this does not constitute an endorsement of them nor a rejection of those that are not named. I have named certain funds either because they are very well known or because they are reasonably representative of a certain category of funds. I have included addresses solely as a service to the reader. You can learn the names, addresses and records of other funds by checking various reports, such as _Investment Companies,_ put out by Wiesenberger Services Inc. These reports are commonly available in brokers' offices and public libraries.

load funds specializing in corporate bonds. They are known as B–1, B–2 and B–4.

The B–1 fund is the most conservative of the Keystone group. Ordinarily, it keeps a considerable portion of its assets in bonds issued by the United States government and its agencies or bonds rated AAA, almost all of the rest in bonds rated AA or A. Its annualized yield, as of late April 1974, was 7.63 percent.

The B–2 fund is less conservative and invests primarily in bonds rated A or BBB. Its annualized yield, as of the above period, was 7.84 percent.

The B–4 fund invests almost exclusively in discount bonds, including some rated BBB and some with lower ratings. Because of the comparatively low ratings of many of its holdings, it enjoys or suffers from much wider fluctuations in its net asset value than B–1 or B–2. In short, although it is riskier than B–1 or B–2, it tends to provide a better yield and a better chance of capital appreciation. Its annualized yield, as of the period cited, was 8.39 percent.

CONVERTIBLE BOND FUNDS

These funds, of course, invest most of their assets in convertible bonds and convertible preferred stocks. As we saw in Chapter 6, convertibles tend to return less income than most other kinds of bonds. But they also provide much more chance for capital gains.

By far the best known of such funds is the Harbor Fund, 1888 Century Park East, Los Angeles, California 90067. This open-end, load fund has been in existence since 1956.

As a matter of policy, it seeks to keep at least 50 percent of its assets, exclusive of cash and government securities, invested in convertible securities. As a matter of practice, it often keeps far more. For example, at the end of one recent year, more than 94 percent of its assets were tied up in convertible bonds, preferred stocks and units.*

For many shareholders, the fund has done well. For example, if you had invested $10,000 in it at the beginning of 1963, reinvested all the dividends you received in the ensuing ten-year period and taken all capital gains distributions in further shares of the fund, your holdings would have been worth slightly more than $26,000 by the end of 1972.

But the roller coaster can go down as well as up. If you had then retained these holdings, they would have declined in value by more than $3,500 in the first six months of 1973.

How about yield? Over the ten and one-half year period in question, it ranged from an average annual low of 3.82 percent to an average annual high of 6.78 percent. Usually, it ranged between 4 and 5.5 percent.

MUNICIPAL BOND FUNDS

There are a raft of these funds. Merrill Lynch, Pierce, Fenner & Smith and John Nuveen & Co. are the leaders in the field. But a number of other brokerage houses sponsor such funds, too, sometimes jointly, sometimes individually. A partial list of such houses includes Bache & Co., E.F. Hutton & Co., Paine, Webber, Jackson & Curtis and Reynolds Securities Inc.

Almost invariably, municipal bond funds are unit trusts sold on a load basis. The load is usually either 3.5 or 4.5 percent of the initial purchase order, depending on the trust.

An investor buys one or more units from such a trust, whose holdings are firmly fixed from the start. Over the

---

*A unit is a stock, stock right or warrant attached to a bond.

Cpt 11 (cont) 145

years, of course, the trusts will gradually shrink in size as the bonds they own are called in or mature and their owners receive their prorated share of return of principal. Interestingly, these trusts usually pay interest monthly rather than semiannually.

When first conceived it was believed the trusts would attract small investors. That's because they usually require minimum investments of only $1,000 or $5,000. But they have proved almost as popular with larger investors. Thus Harry Nielsen, vice president and national marketing manager for John Nuveen & Co., reports that his firm makes about 40 percent of its sales to individuals who invest upward of $50,000.

In addition to these trusts, you may run across a special kind of municipal bond fund that invests only in bonds issued by a particular state or its cities or various public authorities. Obviously, these funds appeal especially to residents of the state in question. That's because the income the residents receive is normally exempt from all federal, state and local income taxes. Residents of other states will not usually have their income exempted from the taxes imposed by and in their own states.

One of the best-known sponsors of such funds is First of Michigan Corporation, Buhl Building, Detroit, Michigan 48226. It periodically brings out unit trusts very similar to those described earlier. Virtually all the assets of these trusts are invested in bonds originating in the State of Michigan.

The load on the trusts is 4.5 percent. The minimum initial investment is $1,000.

Manley, Bennett, McDonald & Co., same address as above, is a newer entry in the field. It sponsors various series of the Michigan Municipal Bond Fund.

Similarly, Merrill Lynch sponsors funds that invest only in bonds put out in Michigan, New York or Pennsylvania.

And E.F. Hutton sponsors funds that invest almost exclusively in bonds put out in California, Michigan, New York or Pennsylvania.

Later, I'll have more to say about the advantages and disadvantages of bond funds in general. Suffice it to say here that, although state bond funds obviously have great appeal to the residents of particular states, questions have been raised about the ability of these funds to find a sufficient number of quality bonds that return good yields.

This criticism may or may not be pertinent to the state bond funds already in existence, which, after all, involve large, heavily populated states. But it clearly seems pertinent to smaller, more sparsely populated states. These states simply may not issue a sufficient number of quality bonds to warrant a special fund.

F. Douglas Harrell, sales manager of the bond funds department of Merrill Lynch, Pierce, Fenner & Smith, says the state funds have tended to yield slightly less than general municipal bond funds. On the other hand, the added tax exemptions often more than make up the difference in yields.

GOVERNMENT BOND FUNDS

These funds invest not only in securities issued by the U. S. Treasury, but also in those issued by federal agencies like Fannie Mae and Ginnie Mae. The two best-known funds are Fund for U.S. Government Securities, Inc., Federated Investors Building, 421 Seventh Avenue, Pittsburgh, Pennsylvania 15219 and Franklin U.S. Government Securities Series, Franklin Custodian Funds, 99 Wall Street, New York, New York 10005.

The Fund for U.S. Government Securities confines itself exclusively to investing in government and agency issues. But the composition of its holdings, among short-term, intermediate-term and long-term issues, may vary at any given point in time.

The fund has proved popular for a number of reasons. It invests only in the safest securities. It requires a minimum initial investment of only $250. It charges a load of only 1.5 percent. And it has had a respectable record.

Its net asset value fell only about 9 percent in the first four and two-thirds years of its life ending June 30, 1974, a drop that is not surprising in view of what has happened to bond prices in recent years. And its average annual yield has been well over 7 percent. It's only fair to add, however, that this yield is somewhat less than that of certain other funds, which invest in different kinds of securities.

HYBRID FUNDS

Perhaps the best example of this kind of fund is the Capital Preservation Fund, Inc., 459 Hamilton Avenue, Palo Alto, California 94301.

This open-end, no-load fund is a hybrid because of its philosophy and practices. Its stated purpose is to keep at least 50 percent of its assets invested in United States government securities at all times. Yet these may be short-term, intermediate-term or long-term securities. And in periods of extreme uncertainty, they may consist entirely of short-term government securities and cash. In better weather, on the other hand, up to one-half of its assets may be invested in corporate bonds—yet only those rated AAA or AA.

When it began operations in October 1972 it had much of its assets in long-term government and corporate bonds. But in ensuing months, the prices of these bonds fell. So in July 1973 it switched its entire portfolio to short-term securities—principally U.S. Treasury tax-anticipation bills, plus a sizable number of certificates of deposit and bankers' acceptances. As this is written, it is still invested in this fashion, but is ready to return to long-term securities whenever conditions warrant. In its short life, it has tended to return slightly more than 7 percent annually.

MONEY-MARKET FUNDS

The oldest of these funds is the Reserve Fund, Inc., 1301 Avenue of the Americas, New York, New York 10019. It came into being early in 1973 and very soon ran up against at least two important imitators: Dreyfus Liquid Assets, 767 Fifth Avenue, New York, New York 10022 and Money Market Management, 421 Seventh Avenue, Pittsburgh, Pennsylvania 15219. As this is written, more than thirty other funds have come into being.

By definition, money-market investments are short-term investments that often mature in no more than one year. As a result, all of the funds invest exclusively in United States government or agency securities, bank certificates of deposit, bankers' acceptances, and commercial paper.

The kicker is that they are able to invest in certain instruments that are beyond the reach of the typical investor. Example: they can buy short-term certificates of deposit, which cannot be purchased in units of less than $100,000.

All three are open-end, no-load funds, and all three have got off to good starts. Thus, in its first twelve months in business, Money Market Management had an average net yield of 9.87 percent, in the next eight an average of 6.26 percent.

Most money-market funds are worth consideration, especially by people who want to invest for short periods of time. The big drawback to the funds is that their yields are directly tied to short-term interest rates, which can fluctuate greatly.

As you can see, there are a great many bond or equivalent funds, and they come in considerable variety. Whatever their precise nature, they all possess certain inherent advantages in common. Among others:

- *Diversification.* Diversifying one's holdings is almost always a sound investment principle. Yet, in the case of bonds, it's not always easy to apply. They cost so much that the small investor may not be able to afford more than two or three of them. Obviously, bond funds provide a way around this impasse. And the diversification they offer is sometimes vertical as well as horizontal. As James M. Benham, chairman and president of Capital Preservation Fund, puts it: "Many attractive bonds and money-market instruments that provide higher than average yields are available only in denominations of $10,000, $25,000 or even $100,000. This puts them beyond the reach of all but the wealthy. But it does not put them beyond the reach of people who invest in bond funds."

- *Professional management.* "This can be even more important in bonds than in stocks," says Michael Lipper, president of Lipper Analytical Services, which keeps track of all kinds of funds. "That's because there is less room for error. Bond prices are largely tied to supply and demand, which in turn are tied to interest rates and the credit-worthiness of bond issuers."

- *Relative safety.* Few funds invest in bonds with ratings lower than BBB. Some have the majority of their holdings in bonds or other debt securities rated AAA, AA or A.

- *Marketability.* Except in the case of closed-end funds, you can almost always sell a fund's shares back to its sponsor. This doesn't necessarily provide protection against dimunition in net asset value. But it does guarantee that you will be able to unload your shares if and when you want to.

- *Convenience.* If you buy into a fund, you won't have to watch for bonds that are called in before maturity. You won't have to hold onto your bonds or safeguard them. You won't have to clip coupons and turn them in for payment. The funds will do all these things for you and mail you checks semiannually, quarterly or often monthly.

- *Two-way protection.* Many people who have invested in bonds or bond funds in recent years would have invested in stocks if the stock market hadn't performed in such lackluster fashion. Now, at least, a few fund sponsors are coming to the rescue of such investors. These companies encourage investors to buy into bond funds, then allow them to invest their interest payments and capital distributions, if any, into stock funds run by the very same companies. By following this procedure, investors gain considerable protection for their original investments, yet enjoy a chance to reinvest their interest with an eye to better capital gains than the bond market can normally provide.

All of these advantages are worth pondering. Yet some are not as important as they may seem. For example, diversification is probably less important to a bondholder than a stockholder. That's because the former can achieve maximum safety by buying only top-rated bonds. In fact, he can achieve even more safety than some of the funds promise. That's because they often buy bonds with less than triple-A ratings.

In this connection, some of the funds have come under fire because of the nature of their holdings. For example, in an article published by *Barron's* in its February 25, 1974,

issue, David Herships, who is in the municipal bond department of Hayden, Stone, took the municipal bond funds in
particular to task.

Said Herships: "The evidence suggests that [fund]
managers . . . may be 'reaching for yield' by purchasing
low-grade issues with below-average marketability and
above-average risk of default. The motivations for seeking
the highest possible returns are to cover the load and en-
hance the funds' sales appeal . . .

"Wall Street is desperately seeking new products. Tax-
exempt bond fund offerings, however, seem a clear-cut
case for liberal application of the warning 'caveat emp-
tor.' "*   Let the buyer beware.

Counters Merrill Lynch's Douglas Harrell: "I know of
no municipal bond funds that contain any bonds rated
lower than BBB. Furthermore, the bonds in these funds are
regularly evaluated by independent outside experts like
Standard & Poor's. Perhaps most important of all, the potential marketability of some of these bonds is irrelevant.
They are not purchased to be traded, but to be held until
they are called in or mature. If any ever defaulted, it would
reflect very badly on the sponsor and any future bond funds
it issued."

Although unit trusts cannot trade their holdings, many
other bond funds can and do trade, sometimes leveraging
in the process. Obviously, they are seeking capital appreciation as well as good income.

Yet several veteran observers question whether the
country possesses enough experienced bond-portfolio
managers to supervise all the funds effectively. Perhaps
more important, these observers question whether even
the most astute managers can profitably trade bonds over
an extended period of time.

And what about yields? If interest rates should fall

*Reprinted by permission of *Barron's* magazine.

sharply and bond prices rise, many funds might be hard pressed to maintain high yields without buying issues of relatively low quality.

The fact is, most probably would not purchase low-quality issues but would allow yields to decline instead. Concedes Merrill Lynch's Harrell: "By and large, the bond funds will reflect the performance of the bond market as a whole."

In this connection, it's well to bear in mind that most bond funds are quite new—some very new. They have not been tested over a period of time that has included major cyclical variations in interest rates. They have been in business in a time when interest rates have generally been rising.

The mutual fund industry may provide a partial analogy. Relatively few mutual funds that invest in common stocks have done consistently well over long periods of time. Those that have been near the top of the pack one year have often been far back two or three years later.

Of course, most bond funds are not as performance-oriented as mutual funds are—that is, they do not make capital appreciation their major goal. They can be expected to concentrate on seeking good income.

Even so, bond funds suffer from other disadvantages. A person who buys bonds directly can pick those with the exact maturities he wants. A person who invests in funds can't do this.

Also, not all of the load funds scale down their sales charges for large investors. The person who buys $100,000 worth of shares may pay just as much, relatively speaking, as the person who buys $1,000 or $5,000.

Even when this is not the case, the cost of buying into some load funds eats heavily into the first year's returns. Indeed, the investor has to hold onto his shares for several years in order to amortize its sales charge to any reasonable degree.

What's more, the investor may achieve a higher yield by investing on his own. Thus even Frank P. Wendt, president of John Nuveen & Co., concedes that an investor may gain as much as a percentage point more yield by making his own purchases.

Finally, there is no universally accepted standard against which bond funds may be compared. To be sure, several prestigious Wall Street firms have formulated bond indices. But, fairly or unfairly, many of these indices have been criticized on the grounds that they cover too few issues, concentrate too heavily on certain kinds of issues, or are based on bond prices that are not totally accurate.

By contrast, mutual funds can be compared not only against their industry's average, but also against the Dow-Jones industrial average and Standard & Poor's 500-stock index. It may be argued, of course, that the Dow-Jones average is not universally accepted, any more than the bond indices are. In fact, it has frequently been called unrepresentative of the stock market as a whole. But if it is not universally accepted, it is almost universally used.

These, then, are the major advantages and disadvantages of bond funds. On balance, how do they stack up? Are they worth the candle?

"Yes," says Henry Kaufman, a general partner of Salomon Brothers and one of the most respected economists in the country. "Bond funds provide a way for the individual to participate in the bond market without having to shop around for individual issues, and they are convenient for other reasons as well. Nonetheless, any investor should carefully study the prospectus of any particular fund to find out the degree of diversification he will get and the quality of the investment the fund will make."

And there is the nub of it. Bond funds do deserve consideration. But like any other investment, they also demand caution and investigation. What exactly should you look for?

154/

Cht. 11

Certainly, you should look at the nature of any given fund in terms of your own desires and needs. Is it a load or no-load fund? Is it an open-end fund, closed-end fund or unit trust? Does it specialize in corporate bonds, municipal bonds or some other kind of debt security?

How does its nature affect its return? For example, if it's a load fund, by how much will its sales charge reduce your yield if this charge is spread over, say, three years? If it's a government fund, how much lower is its yield likely to be than that from a corporate fund?

You should also check the quality of its holdings. Be wary of funds containing a lot of bonds rated lower than BBB. This doesn't mean that funds that own only bonds rated BBB or better are totally safe. It merely means that BBB should be the minimum rating you should expect, unless you deliberately decide to invest in a more speculative fund like Keystone's B-4.

You should also check a fund's maximum turnover rate, unless, of course, it is a unit trust. A turnover rate of 100 percent means the fund's entire portfolio may be replaced within a year. A turnover rate of 300 percent means the entire portfolio may be replaced three times a year. As we have seen, there are both advantages and disadvantages to high turnover rates. What is important is that you understand and accept any given fund's policy on trading.

Check, too, a fund's total expenses. The lower they are, the more that will be left to pay shareholders. Ordinarily, these expenses do not exceed 1.5 percent of annual average net assets and are often considerably less.

In short, bond funds merit consideration. But before you buy into one, learn what kind of fund it is. Ascertain what its past record has been. And recognize that, in the world of investments, there is rarely such a thing as a sure thing.

End of Chpt. 11

Chapter 12

A Few Words of Advice

Scattered through these pages have been various bits of advice designed to help you evaluate different kinds of bonds and buy and sell them to maximum advantage. Now let's recapitulate the most important parts of this advice and add some further pointers.

All these pointers are merely suggestions. They are probably valid for most people most of the time. But don't hesitate to disregard them if they do not apply to your circumstances in any given instance.

First a few dos:

Deal with brokerage houses that have big bond departments. Because they maintain large and varied inventories of bonds, these houses can usually get a better deal for you than most small houses can.

Also, they are more apt to have sizable research staffs.

These staffs will be of great aid to your broker if he is not as familiar with bonds as he is with stocks. In fact, some houses require their brokers to consult with their bond departments before selling bonds to individuals.

You may also want to check with your bank, especially if it is among the nation's biggest. Big banks often maintain sizable bond inventories and conceivably may do even better by you than a brokerage house will.

In fact, it is wise to shop around among several sources before buying bonds. This can be particularly important if a bank or other dealer is a market-maker—that is, if it buys and sells certain securities for its own account and maintains an inventory in them. You may or may not do better elsewhere. All the same, don't be so concerned over the spread or commission you have to pay that you disregard all other factors, such as the kind of organization you are dealing with, the nature of the bond you are considering, its rating and so forth.

Buy with definite goals in mind. There's no point in investing in bonds or anything else without knowing precisely what your aim is and how you can best achieve it.

Are you seeking capital gains? There's nothing necessarily wrong with investing in bonds with this aim in mind, provided you remember that they are not ordinarily considered the best means of achieving capital gains.

Are you seeking income? How much do you require and for what purpose will you use it? When will you need your principal back?

Narrowing your goals will help both you and your broker decide on the right kind of bonds for you. For example, if you will need your principal back in ten years, then you can limit your selection to bonds that will mature in ten years.

In this connection, you should be aware that, by and large, it is much easier to choose among bonds than among

stocks. Even if you limit your choice by several criteria—
kind of bond, rating, yield, maturity and so forth—you will
usually find a number of different issues that will meet your
needs. But it's important to establish these criteria before
you start buying.

Buy bonds that are clearly marketable—those that you
can sell easily and at a decent price should the need arise.
You don't know what the future will hold.

To assure yourself of marketability, avoid bonds from
issues of less than $50 million. If you want to do even more
to assure marketability, confine yourself to bonds rated
AAA or AA, or to government or agency issues. Finally,
suggests First Boston's Charles Walsh, you could limit your
choice to bonds listed on a major exchange. They are more
apt to be marketable in small amounts than bonds sold over
the counter, although this does not hold true, of course, for
municipals, almost all of which are sold in that fashion.

If you want to buy municipals, give serious consideration to buying those issued by or in your own state. This
advice is particularly appropriate if you live in a large,
heavily populated state that is likely to have many different
bonds. By buying such bonds, you will very likely avoid
all state and local income taxes and thus increase your
yield.

This does not necessarily mean that you should confine
yourself to bonds issued in your own state. After all, diversification is usually a sound principle to follow.

Buy new bonds. Some dealers insist that you will do
better to buy seasoned issues. And in some cases, they may
be right. But there is at least one clear-cut advantage to
buying new issues. More time will have to elapse before
they become subject to call. Therefore, you will be sure of
earning interest for a longer period of time.

Review your portfolio annually, whatever its composition. Circumstances do change. You may be single one

year, married the next, or married, then widowed. You may have a new child, a new home or a new job. Even if your life has undergone no changes, you should review your portfolio each and every year. New developments may affect your bonds or the bond market in general. It's true that bonds are usually bought for the long term. Even so, you should never consider yourself irretrievably wedded to a particular security.

And now for a few don'ts:

Avoid bonds that will be subject to wide fluctuations in price. Obviously, this should not be a hard-and-fast rule. In fact, you probably won't be able to observe it at all if you invest in convertible bonds.

But if there's any chance at all that you will have to sell your bonds before they mature, you must give this rule some weight. Aside from convertibles, the bonds most apt to fluctuate in price are those that will mature well in the future, those that offer yields that are higher than the going rate right from the start and those that carry low rates of interest.

Obviously, if you apply this rule, you may have to give up one advantage—say, a yield higher than the going rate —in order to obtain another—namely, some price stability. So, more than most, this factor should be weighed together with others, not considered all by itself.

Avoid bonds subject to early call, especially if they carry high rates of interest. Otherwise, you may own your invest-ment only a relatively short period of time.

Avoid bonds that are selling for more than their call prices. If they should be called in, you could suffer a loss of capital.

Avoid bonds that have been issued by new companies. Such companies have no track records and for that reason their bonds may be unrated. Even if this is not the case, you'll do well to stick to bonds issued by companies that have been in business a number of years.

Avoid delaying your investments until you think interest rates have hit their peak. This doesn't mean you should give no consideration at all to rising interest rates. But trying to buy bonds when interest rates are at their very crest is like trying to buy or sell a stock when it hits its bottom or reaches its top. Few people are able to pick the exact day when stock prices hit their precise lows or highs —or when interest rates reach their very zenith.

Avoid bonds with low ratings unless you definitely want to speculate. This means you should not buy bonds with ratings of less than triple-B. And if safety of principal is extremely important to you, you should make your cut-off rating even higher—probably double-A.

Avoid margining to the hilt. If your bonds fall in price, you may have to put up more money at a time when it is inconvenient. And bear in mind that it rarely pays to buy municipals on any margin at all. The interest on the loan will not be tax-deductible.

Finally, never forget the most important fundamental facts about bonds and the bond market. First, their chief and most common advantage is that they usually provide— or should provide—good income. Second, their chief and most common disadvantage is that they are not inflation-proof—or, to be more exact in this day of high interest rates, they are only partially inflation-proof. Third, they should probably not be bought as a substitute for stocks. If you do buy them when the stock market is languishing, with the thought that you will later return to stocks, you should probably confine your choice to bonds with short maturities or to money-market instruments like U.S. Treasury bills. Fourth, never forget that bonds are bought and sold in a market dominated by and geared to large institutional investors.

This is changing somewhat. And it may change even

more. But it is not likely to change so much that institutions will still not dominate the market and help govern everything that takes place in it.

All this reinforces the importance of weighing an investment in bonds just as carefully as you would weigh one in stocks or real estate or anything else. As they say, investigate before you invest.

End of chpt. 12

_(167)_

(S) cont.   _(T) cont._   Index **167**

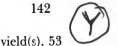

End of Index

168

Catalog

If you are interested in a list of fine Paperback
books, covering a wide range of subjects
and interests, send your name and address,
requesting your free catalog, to:

McGraw-Hill Paperbacks
1221 Avenue of Americas
New York, N.Y. 10020